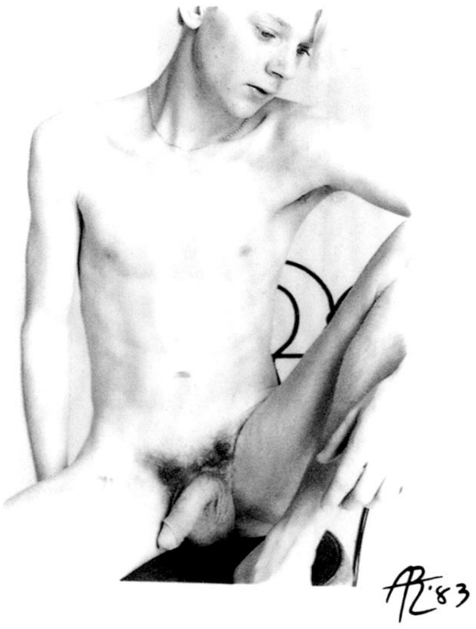

Temptations
of
St. Anthony

BALTIMORE Portraits

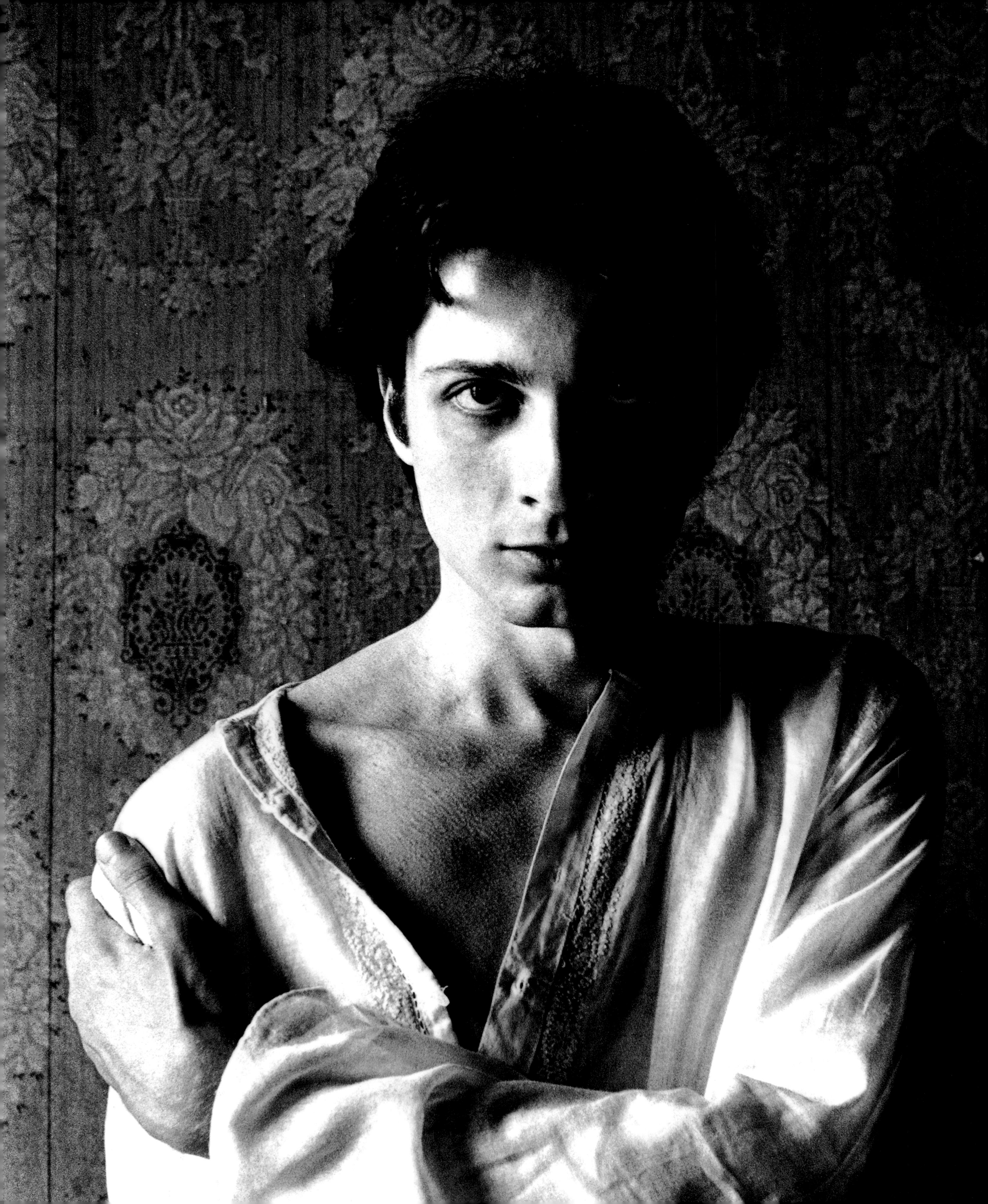

Amos Badertscher

Baltimore Portraits

Introduction by Tyler Curtain

Published by Duke University Press

Durham & London

In association with

Duke University Museum of Art

1999

Contributors

The publication of this book has been made possible by a generous grant from the Hanks Endowment. Additional support has been provided by the following contributors:

Mr. A. E. Badertscher
Mr. F. Dean Badertscher
Mr. Jeffrey A. Bugenhagen
Mr. and Mrs. Harry S. Bullen III
Mr. Rodney Y. Corbin
Mr. James Cummings
Mr. Ronald R. Decarlo
Mr. Mark A. Emmel
Ms. Margaret A. Fiore
Ms. Marilyn H. Gabor
Mr. and Mrs. Albert M. Harris
Ms. Ann K. Luard
Mr. Larry M. Magee
Ostafin Design
Mr. Robert B. Riefler
Mr. John M. Sharpe
Mr. Paul Sharpe
Mr. Scott M. Shaver
Ms. Cynthia Surgeon
Mr. John F. Thompson, Jr.
Mr. Robert W. Tully
Dr. Anthony Venbrux
Mr. James Zitzer, Jr.

This book is especially for Michael Mezzatesta,
Frank Degen and Gary Scharfman of Degen/Sc
and William, my companion for 15 years.

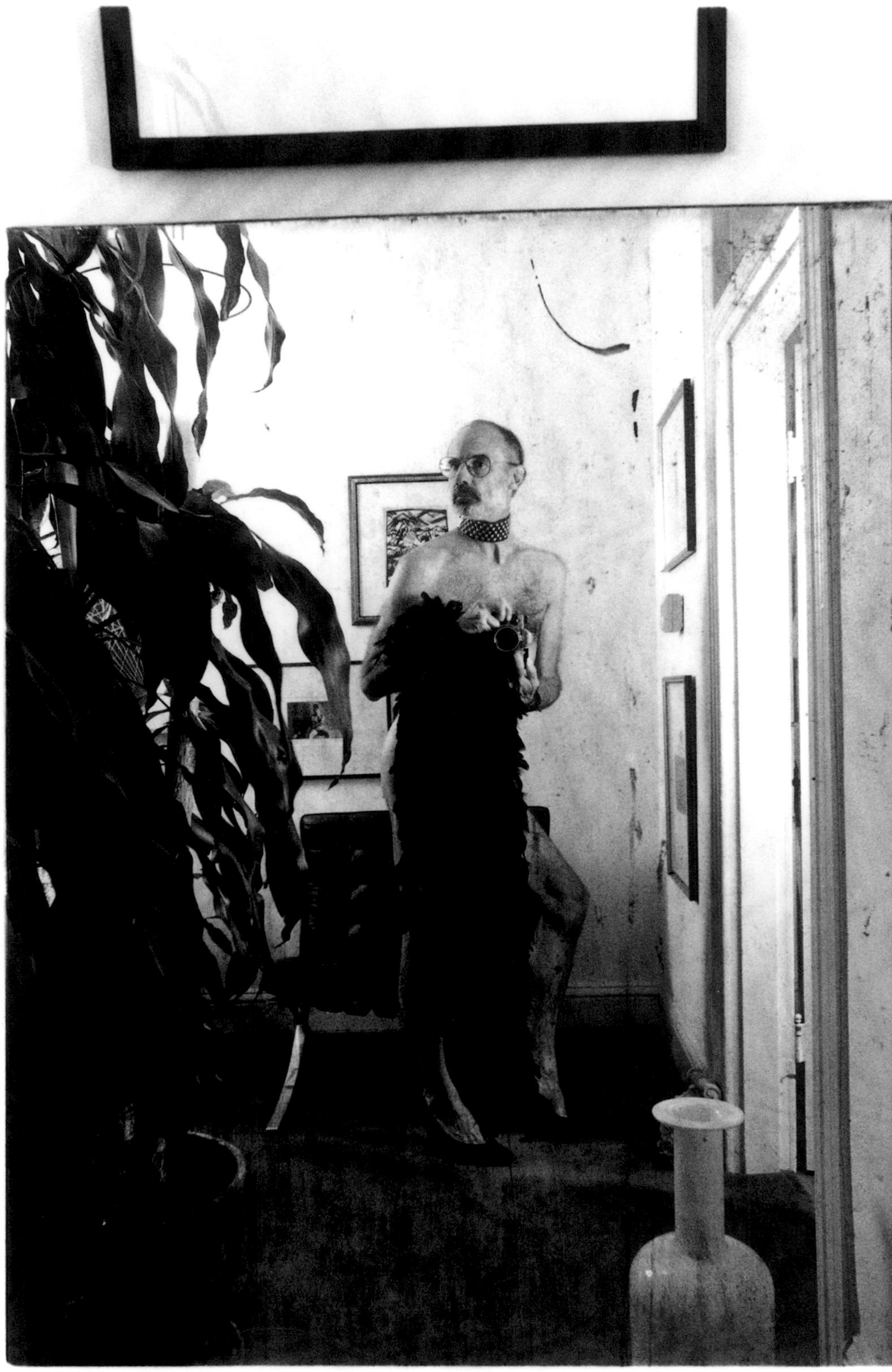

Self Portrait with boa

AC '93

Power dressing

Father of Otters, it is himself!

Finnegans Wake
p. 214

Foreword

Michael P. Mezzatesta
D.B.T. and James H. Semans Director
Duke University Museum of Art

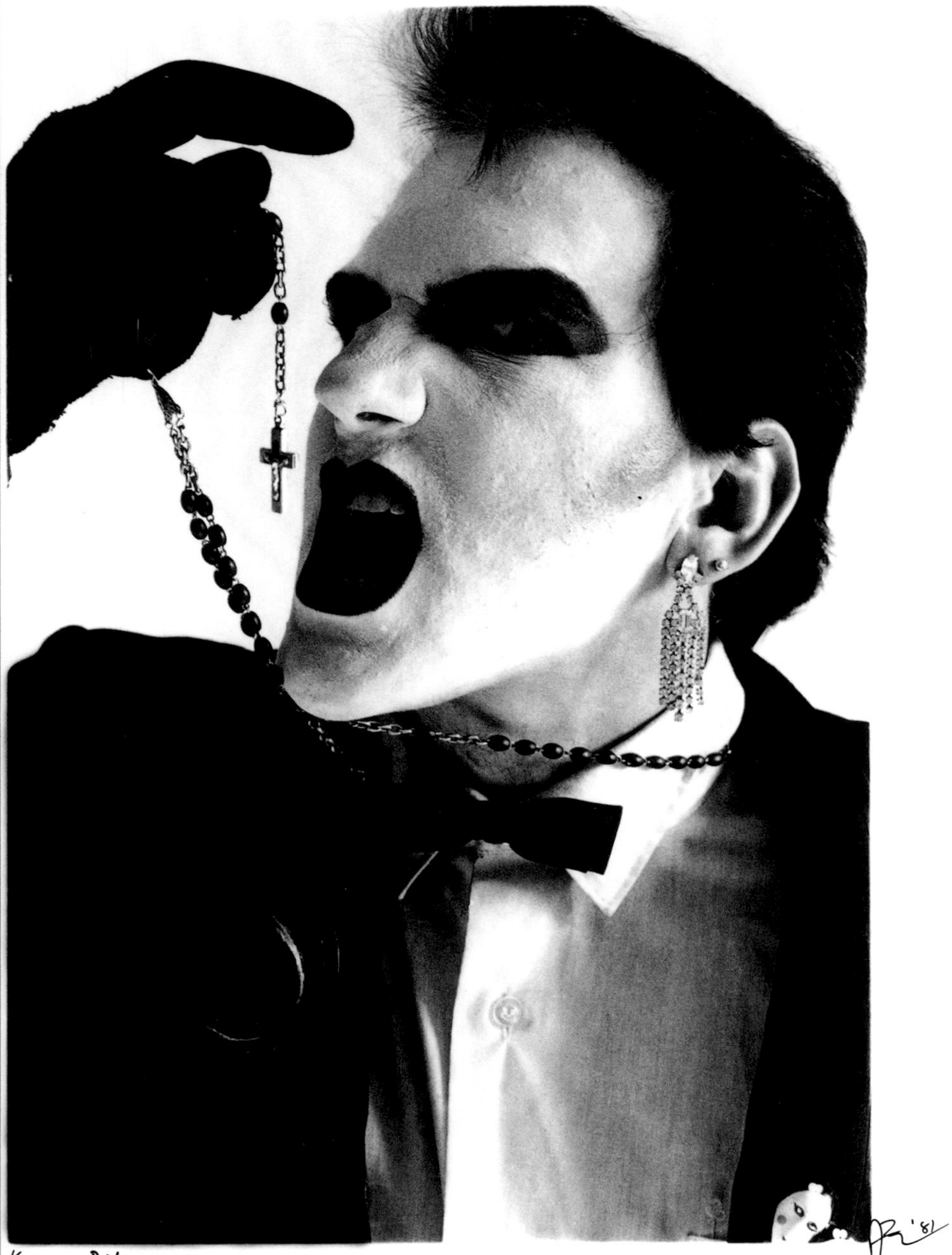

Kerry Riley
Baltimore portrait: 1981. A kinder, gentler America.

A young man wearing a cheap tuxedo jacket, whiteface and makeup, and a rhinestone earring dangling, fixes us with an angry confrontational stare as, with a black-gloved hand, he lowers a rosary into his gaping mouth. This shockingly aggressive and provocative image—seen above and ironically entitled—*Baltimore Portrait: 1981. A kinder, gentler America*—perfectly encapsulates the story that Amos Badertscher tells about his hometown. It has provided the title to this book.

Since the 1970s self-taught photographer Amos Badertscher has created images of Baltimore's subculture, a slice of urban life that has rarely been documented let alone acknowledged by artists or mainstream institutions. His subjects are people on the margins of society: prostitutes, teenage hustlers, transvestites, drug users, strippers, nightcrawlers, wannabe rockstars.

Photographed in his studio, in the city's night clubs and gay bars, beneath bridges and highway underpasses, his work forms a remarkable chronicle, an archival record of a city and its illicit fringe culture.

The photographer is not, however, a dispassionate observer, for his work is autobiographical. This is his world and these are his people. Through bold images accompanied by text inscriptions—calligraphically rendered biographies that read like short prose poems, condensing the essence of an often tragic life into a few stark sentences—he recounts their stories: young boys who turn tricks for male clients; gender-bending women and men struggling to be themselves; sybaritic odalisques, both horizontal and vertical, displaying their charms. Sadly, as we scan texts that record lives lost to drugs or AIDS, these poignant images all too often reveal themselves as memento mori.

Although some of these photographs have a strong elegiac quality, many others are filled with an incredible joie de vivre. Badertscher captured the exuberance of the denizens of Baltimore's demimonde, their irrepressible assertion of individuality in the face of family and public scorn. Many of these sitters come alive with an in-your-face sexual presence that is often humorous, sometimes antagonistic and threatening, usually outrageous, frequently voyeuristic, and always blatantly assertive. These characters cannot, will not be ignored. Costumed, flaunting, gesturing, posing, posturing, forcing their way into our space and consciousness, they represent a scintillating, idiosyncratic creativity that refuses to be suppressed by middle-class convention. These characters are "on the edge," like the oddball, offbeat eccentrics who populate John Waters's tales of his quirky hometown. Along the lines of Waters, Badertscher presents the "other" Baltimore, the one you never hear about in the travelogues. Peeling away the facade of its neo-Renaissance and its Federal Style civility, Badertscher reveals a darker Baltimore, more complex, diverse, and troubled than the casual visitor might imagine.

Although the subject of Badertscher's lens has been Baltimore, his sitters are hardly unique to that city. They could have been found in thousands of cities across the United States where lives are being lost to substance abuse, family breakups, alcohol, drugs, AIDS, sexual prejudice, and intolerance. As the artist points out, not only is it a tragedy that we are losing these lives, but perhaps the greater tragedy is that no one seems to care. Amos Badertscher has humanized people many of us might never encounter or think about, conveying not only the tragedy of lives lost but also the indomitable drive of the spirit to make itself known.

The work of Amos Badertscher was exhibited at the Duke University Museum of Art (DUMA) in the fall of 1995. This book grew out of that show. Its publication has been made possible by the help of many generous donors who are listed individually on the contributors page. Paul Sharpe did a masterful job in organizing that fund-raising effort. Additional funding was generously provided by Duke University President Nannerl O. Keohane through the Hanks Endowment. Her support is deeply appreciated. I am particularly grateful to Amos for his enduring good humor over the years that it has taken to produce *Baltimore Portraits.* We have both learned the meaning of patience. For me, and I hope for Amos, the final product has been well worth the wait. I am also indebted to Amos for granting the museum permission to tour these works as a traveling exhibition.

Special thanks are extended to Ken Wissoker and Richard Morrison of Duke University Press for their perseverance in helping to make the book a reality and to Tyler Curtain for his fine essay introducing the work—he has done an outstanding job of explaining and contextualizing these works. Finally, I would like to acknowledge Nancy Sears, head of DUMA's public relations and design department, and a nationally recognized book designer. Nancy created this book. It is a work of art in its own right. We are so fortunate to have her working at DUMA.

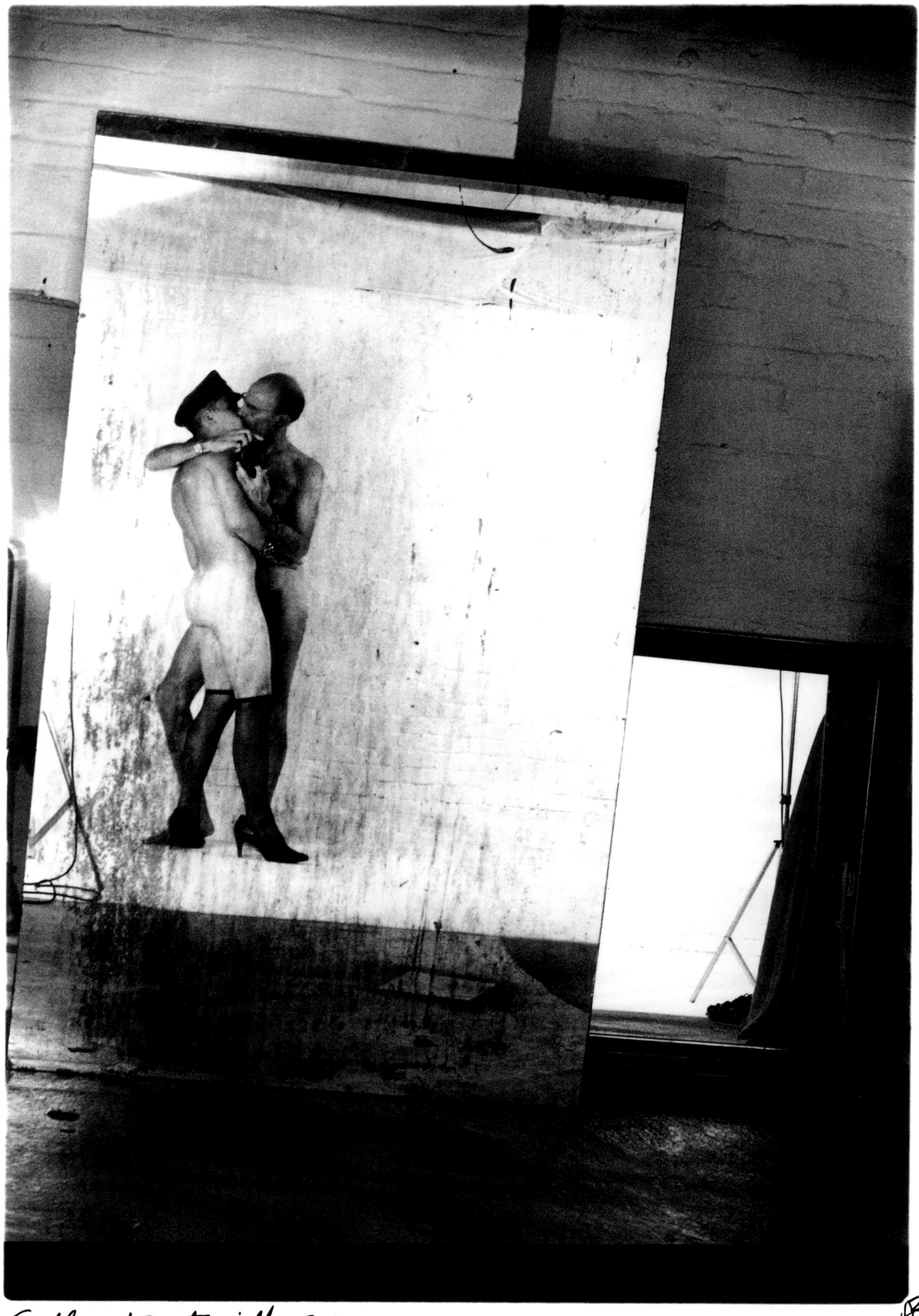

Self-portrait with Steven

JR '95

Yet why not say what happened.

Robert Lowell

I began working with a camera in the mid- to late 1960s, moving from an ancient Polaroid purchased for twenty-five dollars and an Argus C-3 (my mother's wedding gift to my father in 1935) to a more sophisticated instrument. Long fascinated with the photographic image (mostly historical), I set out immediately to photograph the world. Gradually, it became evident that my talents did not lie in a universal direction and as a result of a serendipitous experience I began concentrating exclusively on the male figure. The rest of the world was put on hold.

Photographing the nude figure in the USofA, especially the young male nude, even during the more liberated 70s, was not an innocent or trouble-free undertaking. I was forced to employ a number of eccentric and photogenic friends, gay and otherwise, and the ubiquitous teenagers who sold their bodies at an alarming number of locations throughout Charm City. The middle American family—where sexual suppression is honed to a fine art, thereby ensuring the creation of the highly aggressive male animal necessary for the continuation of a capitalistic, consumerist culture—would have none of my curious explorations.

There must have been something dangerously lacking in my upper-middle-class psyche because I did not find nudity, even youthful male nudity, shocking, abusive, emasculating, pornographic, or subversive. To photograph the naked body is, for me, the ultimate dimension in photographing the person. The way the good father (or god, bless his perverse heart) made it. Genitalia and all the other stuff. The censorabilia according to Jack Smith. The youthful nude, of either sex, captures a beautiful and terribly fragile experience, an innocence that has been the inspiration for many of the great masters of literature, poetry, painting, and sculpture throughout all of Western culture. A few brilliant photographers come to mind: Sally Mann, Jock Sturges, Peter Hujar, Will McBride. And Larry Clark and David Hamilton.

How we have arrived today in America, after *Hair* and *Show Me* and the promising 60s, at such a state of paranoia regarding sex and youthful nudity is a more involved matter for another discussion. Of course, our loudly professed concern for shielding our children (from mother nature?) does not rescue them from gross poverty, abuse, illiteracy, disease, drugs, prostitution, and homelessness. Meanwhile, the saved portion of the social equation obsesses itself with the billionaire next door, the Internet, the Gucci ethic, BMWs, quarter-of-a-million dollar wristwatches, personal trainers, designers and eyebrow pluckers, A-lists, Monica, pedophiles and Deepak Chopra, the candy or gooey guru.

Why the kids are out there on the street and homeless in the first place is a question few are asking. They are certainly not asking this question in Congress or in city councils. Who is responsible for this, you might ask. Certainly not Jock Sturges or his fans; certainly not Will McBride, author of *Show Me,* the most creative sex education book yet devised—banned in the land of the free; certainly not homosexuals or homosexual couples (a joke); certainly not those who ogled those young Calvin Klein models a few years back. The real answer to this problem is too elusive or too painful to contemplate. Its roots are firmly embedded in the latent and active aggression of a capitalist order and in the blindness and bizarre ideology that allows our entire United States Congress and executive branch and Justice Department to sit in a city, just yards from the worst poverty, corruption, and disease in America. You wouldn't have a clue to this state of affairs visiting our awesome shrines of power or listening to the flatulent goings-on on the Senate floor, where the most vital concerns of a day lie in exploring the finer definitions of sexual harassment. So what are we really obsessed with? What is next to God and cleanliness and the World Wide Web? Sex! Of course. Ask any president. But we certainly don't want our youth to witness their nude, or suggestively nude, bodies depicted anywhere, let alone a PENIS. And because of the years and years of media hype augmenting this pervasive abuse hysteria, the young themselves are running as scared as their parents. They already have built-in big brother monitors. To visualize themselves depicted nude would certainly make them gay. To wear a bikini on a beach would make them very gay.

But what about those less fortunate? The tens and tens of thousands of street kids truly growing in numbers as you read this. The ones with no parents or direction or education, with scary diets and hygiene, selling or using any drug imaginable, their knowledge not extending much beyond rap, "the neighborhood," and the nineties. They will not go away. No matter what is not done in Washington or how many verbal or photodocumentaries chronicle their plight. Well, one good solution is to put them in jail. Or those lovely detention centers, overcrowded and understaffed. Those not in custody we can forget. Go after the one-in-a-million pedophiles and pornographers. And David Hamilton and Jock Sturges. Such people are fewer in number and easy to get. You can sue and arrest them. Reaffirm family values. That works every time. Just ask the Christian right and Jesse Helms and Trent Lott and Dan Quayle and the rest of the heavenly choir. The same people who forever want a colossal military budget. Those same Christians who, in the name of a free society, readily withhold medical supplies and life's sustenance from the desperate human beings in Cuba and Iraq. Those whose absolute fascination with porno-Puritanism allows them to conveniently overlook the spectacular and mindless excesses of middle America at Disneyland and Las Vegas. Ignorance and bad taste are not dealt with in Leviticus. And let us not forget the Cincinnati lawyer

Charles Keating, the very conservative founder of Citizens for Decent Literature (whatever that is) convicted at last of seventy-three (73) counts of fraud, racketeering, and conspiracy in defrauding Lincoln Savings and Loan and all of its investors. Just what literature was he reading, if any? Or Randall Terry, the rod of god, whose followers stalk big book stores and tear up books featuring unclad youths. Now, you won't see these people out on city streets trying to care for, educate, rehabilitate, or employ all those children who will certainly die in poverty and drug addiction. They've probably never seen these kids. Just the nude ones in books. The result—other than the very painful and unnecessary wailing and gnashing of teeth on both sides, which spawns an atmosphere for some serious, possibly terrifying, social disorder—is merely a greater curiosity about and sales of the horrific books in question. Finally, let's retire to gated communities (or Celebration, the good-as-it-gets Disney concoction in Florida) and expire in boredom. Being very careful, of course, to keep those tax dollars to ourselves and specifically out of the hands of the corrupt and deranged cities, where they just might need them. The same cities that built this country.

amen

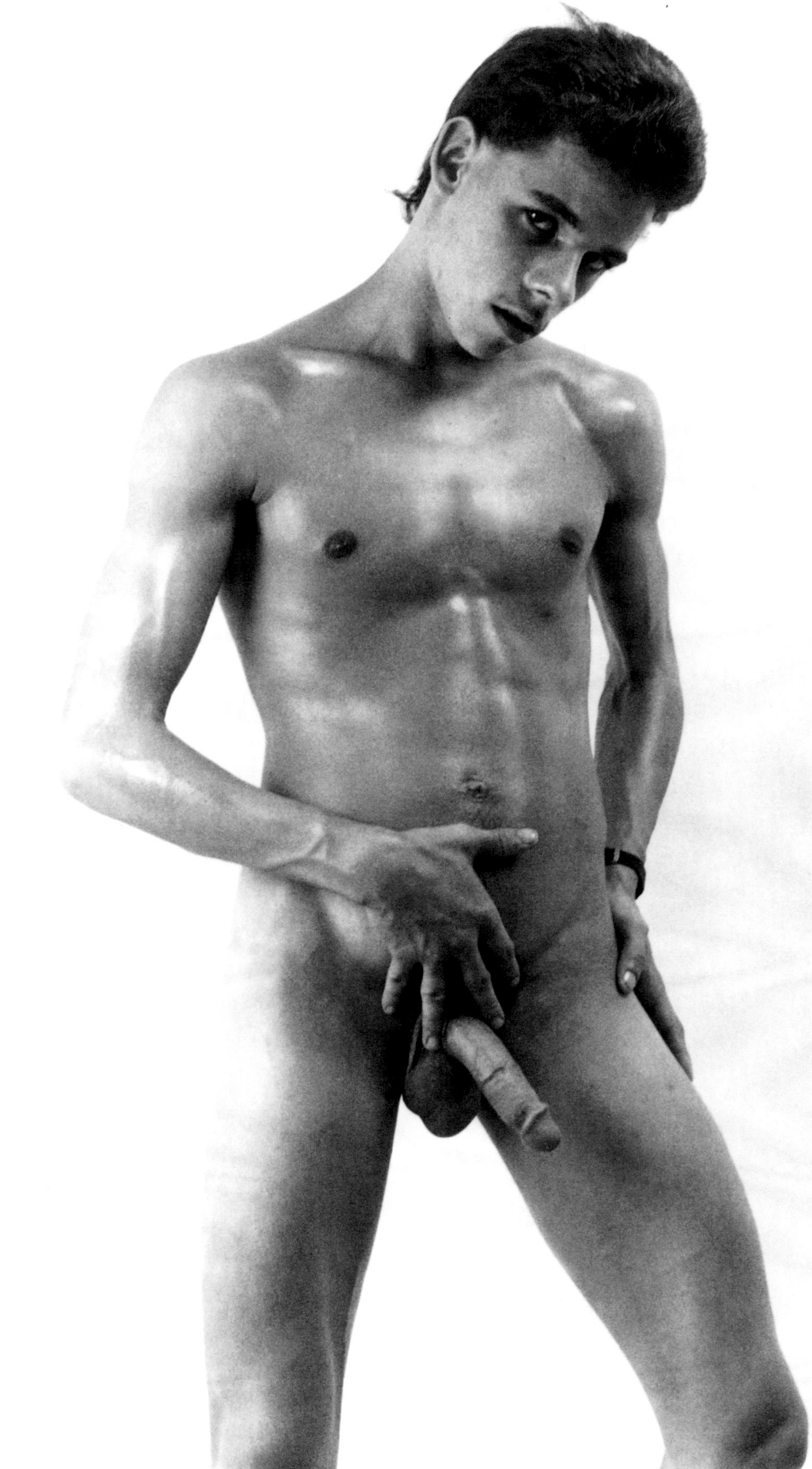

'89

Brian Householder

Brian was one of the more talented dancers at Club Atlantis in Baltimore. He had entertained men in one way or another since the age of ten. This photograph was taken in Oct. of '89, three years before he died of AIDS, at the age of twenty-one.

A BALTIMORE ESSAY: Photography, Sexuality, Community

Tyler Curtain

There's a desperate dynamic to Amos Badertscher's Baltimore photographs: they are intense, angry, pungently erotic. For the past thirty-odd years, Badertscher has used his camera to record prostitutes and hustlers, petty thieves and addicts, drag queens and performance artists, transvestites, strippers, and drug dealers. The people who step into and out of the frames of these photos were his friends, lovers, erotic fixations, acquaintances, tricks, street kids, and pretty boys who wanted attention and affirmation. Badertscher's art takes the feel, the excitement, of a trick and transfers it to the surface of the photo. It's an extraordinary, arresting effect. The photographs perform the intimacy of a crowded gay bar or strip club: immediately sexually charged, when you touch them they discharge the shock of familiarity of the skin of someone you've just met though never known.

The art of this trick is, in part, an artlessness. Badertscher is a self-taught photographer who respects and plays off of the personalities and lives that his subjects bring to his portraits. His photographic sessions aren't elaborately planned and determined by an "auteur," as it were, but are spontaneous, improvisational. The subjects frame themselves within his shots as much as he does, an erotic give and take that comes off on the film.

In the preface to this volume, Badertscher himself explains how he came to his work, something of his process, as well as the themes and concerns his art embodies. Badertscher is acutely aware of the significance of his work within the context of larger social and cultural aesthetics, attitudes, politics, and institutions. He names both the homophobia and the conflicted pedophilia and erotophobia of contemporary society. He names gay and lesbian identity politics as complicitous with the sex panic of recent years. For its own part, the society and attitude that he castigates with such urgency calls his art and erotics immoral.

The morality of Badertscher's extraordinary work seems to me to be beside the point. What I would like to address is what makes these photographs representatively, intensely queer and unrepresentatively respectful of queer folks lives. Male nude photography may enrage and entice its critics, but as Badertscher practices it, it's neither moral nor immoral. The photographs aren't static, sanctimonious, or "straight" pronouncements about the supposed consequences of the lives of the dead. The photographs are ferocious, complex, and dynamic memorials to the ways in which we fight to live.

Admittedly, resisting the impulse to make moral statements about these peoples lives is difficult; the surface anonymity of Badertscher's portraits makes that resistance even more difficult. In many of his works, blank backgrounds accentuate what seems to be a displaced anonymity. However displaced any one of the photographs might feel, though, they are never disembodied. And those bodies come from a very real place. The images take up bits and pieces of the sexual world of Baltimore. That landscape has a few recognizable landmarks that have persisted over the years: Patterson Park, the Block, the gay bars of Mount Vernon, to name only a few of the areas you could pick out on a map of the city, or drive by on an accidental tour. The objects of interest in this terrain, as in Badertscher's art, are the people. Baltimore was once an extraordinarily cruisy town: on a warm evening, you could drive along Park Avenue near Grace and St.

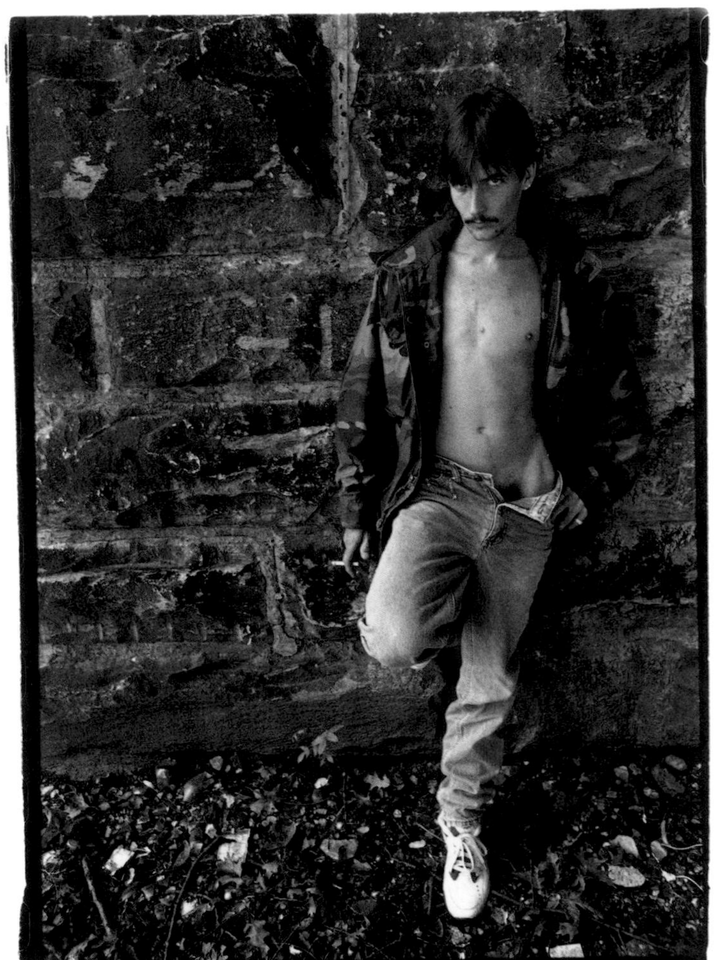

Walt MacNew

Here Walt is 24 yrs. of age. A Remington boy. His father left the family when he was ten and the dominant women in his life were his mother, grand-mother + sister. Like all boys of his class he is "straight" but has been hustling men since 14. Or whatever else it takes to survive.

Peter's Church and lose count of the teenage boys who had come out to make a buck. Badertscher grew up in this world.

Transvestites, prostitutes, and a few young men still stroll late nights and early mornings on Park, but the sexual life has shifted. Disease and drug abuse have taken their toll, as have vice crackdowns and middle-class gentrification. The center of the city is still queer, but it has mellowed and washed out. The patchwork of Baltimore's neighborhoods has frayed. Towson, for instance, is more suburban than urban; Charles Village to Pig Town has gentrified, or at least tried to, given persistent problems with unemployment and poverty. Queer life in the center of the city has taken on the diluted tones of an ad in the *Advocate.* The Polish and Italian working-class rowhouses in and around Fells Point form a rough-trade, mostly white neighborhood on the southeast side of the city, a neighborhood that retains a trace of what sexual life was thirty years ago.

The neighborhoods are trying to hold their own but are decaying nonetheless. The Catholic Church has shut down several churches within the diocese, an action which signals how corrosive the economic and cultural trends are to the city's life. But where the neighborhood is still able to maintain its grip, sexual identity doesn't operate in the same way that it does among the WASPy middle classes. At the Atlantis, a long-time male strip club that sits under a highway overpass in downtown Baltimore, a stone's thrown from Fells Point, few of the dancers self-identify as gay. Those that come from the neighborhood and the working-class outskirts of the city have girlfriends, though they turn men for cash, alcohol, and sometimes drugs. Pulaski Highway boys or Patterson Park kids turn tricks for money. Having sex with men is about a lot of things—authority, abuse, thrills, aspirations, boredom, survival—but it isn't necessarily about identity.

In this sense, then, Badertscher's work is documentary or archival in character. "Here Walt is 24 yrs. of age. A Remington boy." It records the patterns and tones of lives that don't fall into sociological morality tales about the development of "healthy," "gay," "adult" identities. In part, it documents attitudes about self, sexuality, and surroundings that were much more common thirty years ago. The amber of the city has preserved people as they were and, in pockets, are. The people who imprinted traces of themselves on the surface of these photos lived lives that were oriented around desire, pleasure, poverty, authority, self-determination, anger, and need. Often, a damaged, intense affect sculpts the image of the photo.

Such affect makes for at times explosive, at times mesmerizing photography. A constellation of comparable photographers comes to mind as one works through Badertscher's collection: Nan Goldin, Sally Mann, Cindy Sherman, Greg Gorman, Will McBride, Jack Shear, Duane Michals, David Hamilton, not to mention the Larry Clark of *The Perfect Childhood.* One can find parallels in subject and technique in each of these photographers, but what interests me about Badertscher's work are the ways in which he enables his subjects to gel the surface of the photo, which is to say, to contribute to the artistry of the image. Badertscher's photography from the seventies and eighties is certainly prescient of Jack Shear's modes; with no background, unplaced, they anticipate an aesthetic that in Shear's male nudes underlines action and movement but in Badertscher's work absorbs and displays personalities. Shear's floating, kinetic bodies subtract specificity in order to abstract and distill a moment, a movement. His bodies are faceless and in motion. Badertscher's subjects, full of face, tend to challenge the camera, to make it part of themselves. Badertscher pushes against what is anthropological, against making his subjects alien or objectlike. The photograph allows them to speak in the first person. I maintain that this is what makes his work, and work like it, *queer.*[1]

A first-person voice doesn't necessarily mean that one isn't speaking through a persona. The persona one takes on is an integral part of the person one is. By

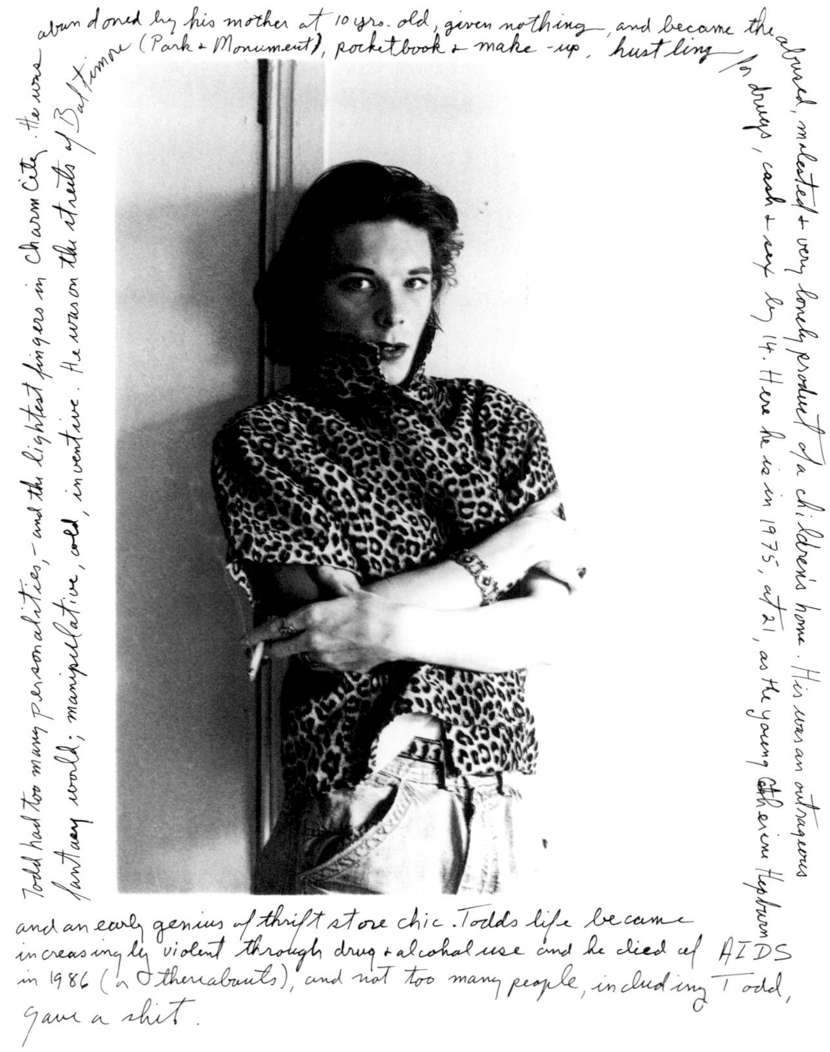

contrast, for instance, Cindy Sherman's photographs are at times like watching someone's slides from their vacation (something like, "here is me in a hat and lederhosen in Germany," translated into, say, "here is me as a teenage Chicano boy," or "here is me as a corpse that has drowned"); the self-consciousness of her personas dissolves any sense that she lives in and through the images that she steps into. Badertscher's images and words, such as "Todd had too many personalities," fuse the shifting, exploratory, desperate, angry, and vulnerable in what amounts to an eggshell fragility and strength of a stare. Todd not only lives in his work, he is his work.

"Here he is in 1975 as the young Catherine [*sic*] Hepburn." Badertscher's commentary allows the life of his subject to spill over into the underlying narrative of the photo. Badertscher records the survivalist's art of living through the strength, self-worth, and self-determination of a movie-star image. In part it is what queer

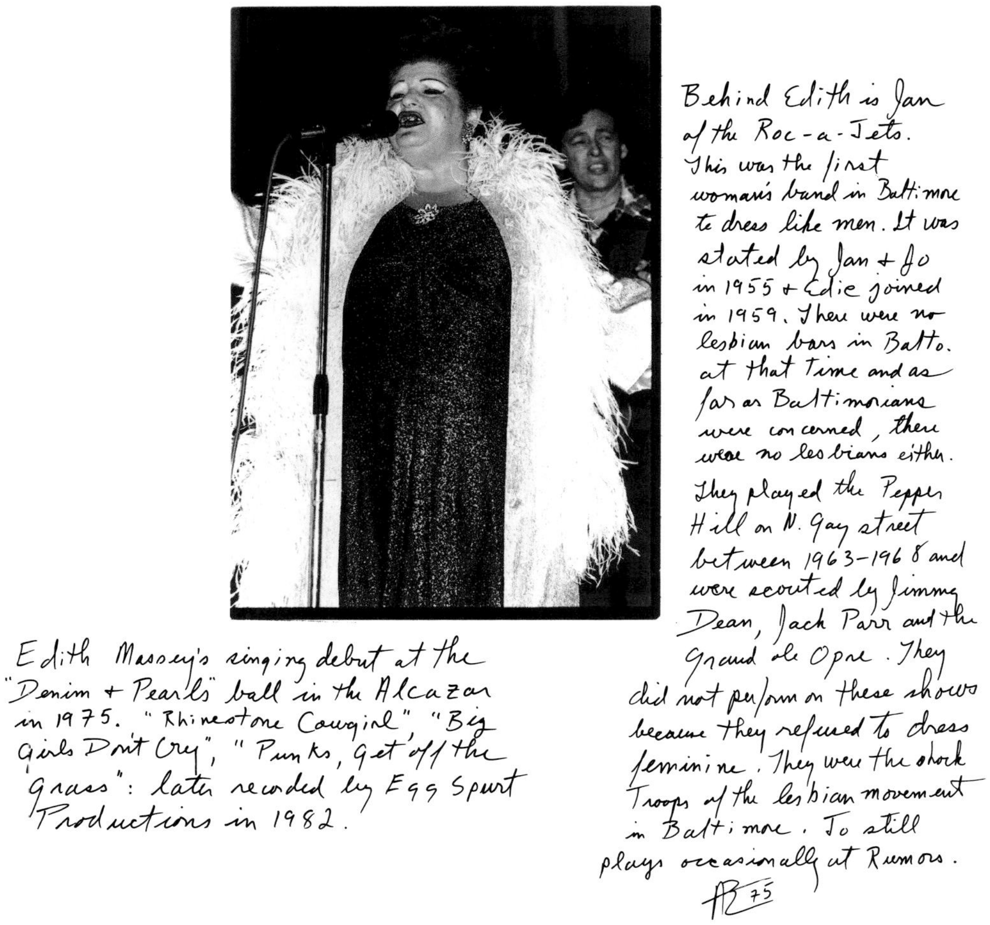

scholar Stephen Oldenberg Barber has called "a mode of joyful experimentation with being" or "the gestural codes of gay bodies—their corporal morphology." It is joyful, but it is a sharp, ragged joy, part of a drag queen's fierceness, a way of shouldering into the world's recognition, if not affirmation. It's the skin of Todd's leopard-skin coat. The stare and the drag demand to be taken into account.

Another example: if you were to contrast Greg Gorman's head shot of John Waters to Badertscher's photograph of Edith Massey—Waters and Massey both being Baltimore natives and underground queer cult figures—the first image seems thin and insubstantial compared to the second. Next to Badertscher, Gorman takes essentially empty photographs, meaning apparently generated by the artistry of the photographer, but more often than not generated by the celebrity of the subject. *I know him, I recognize her* are the only critical statements prompted by Gorman's images. Familiarity is an important function of photographic portraiture, but Gorman's is the familiarity of the fan magazine snapshot that snaps shut any investigation of meaning. Badertscher's art, on the other hand, repositions familiarity within a metaphoric space, akin to Annie Leibowitz's astonishing allegorical work. Leibowitz's image of Whoopi Goldberg in a bathtub of milk, for instance, allows the fame of the subject to help establish the complexities of meanings within the photograph, but doesn't let it act as a buttress that supports all meaning.

Badertscher invites/invests familiarity through the narratives he pens underneath or embeds his photographs within. Literally, this is a story that the artist writes by hand in his photograph's margins. The framing narratives are as much a part of the art as the image itself. Just as his subjects often bleed into and out of the defining white spaces of the photograph, his subjects' lives bleed into the underwritten text. "Frank was born in 1955, the year I graduated from high school" (1) is cut in half by John Yau's "Not even a voice wafer is heard / among the stars' splintered echoes." The bottom image echoes the top; Frank Grundahl's birth and life echo against Badertscher's matter-of-fact punctuation of the image by his death, "in 1992 of AIDS, at 37."

Around Frank's neck are two symbols that were popular pendants in the 1970s: a razor blade and a Saint Christopher's medal. The medal you can see pendant in the middle of Frank's chest. The razor is snug below his Adam's apple. Frank is pinned back by a threat nuzzled against his neck and a promise of protection centered on his chest. The razor itself is a compact package that promises both pleasure and pain; an instrument used to tally cocaine into soft lines that deliver a hard, sharp punch, as well an instrument that threatens to cut one's throat. The Christopher medal is as much a sincere prayer for protection for a kid raised in the heavily Catholic Baltimore as it is an ironic, knowing shrug about the dangers of that city to

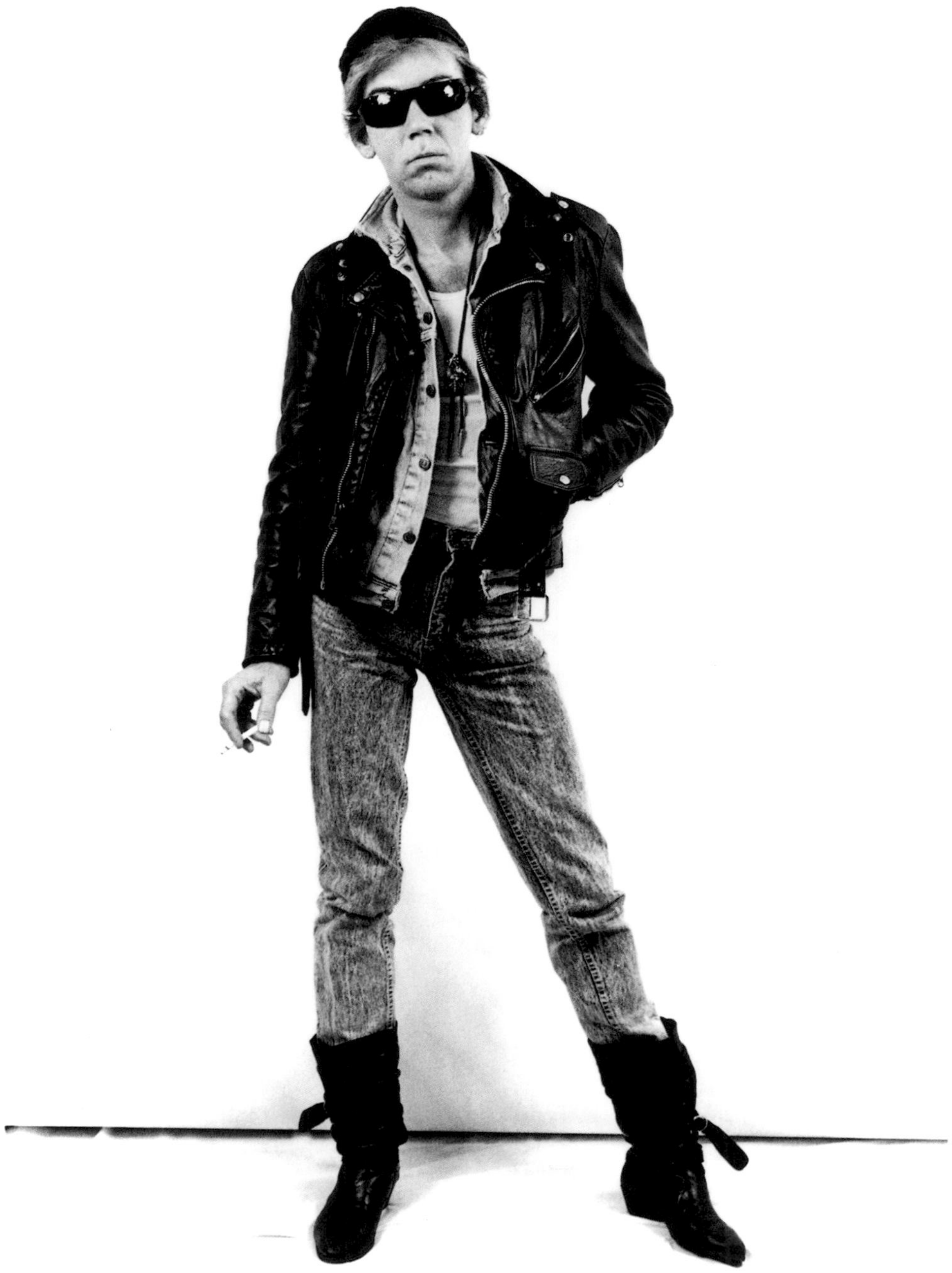

Kenny Zutell (1989), aka Kenny Legs, hit the streets of Baltimore at age 14, 1964. He hustled City Hall square, the White Coffee Pot at Howard + Franklin, Bickfords at Baltimore + St. Paul, Eddies Bar at Light and Water Sts., the corner of Park + Monument by Grace + St. Peters where Miss Todd got her start (divine meat racks) and the fabulous Pepper hill at 213 N. Gay Street within spitting distance from the old Central Police parking lot. He slept with some Hollywood stars playing at local theaters in the 60's + some Baltimore celebrities (he could name names). At 18 he worked for Sugar Sweet in Houston + was run out of Town by the local vice. He was named Kenny Legs by an ancient stripper, May de Carla. Then into his 40's he lived with his mother in Highland Town + held court at the Unicorn on Boston St. Just one of the truly bad, bad girls + a survivor in the grand manner. Kenny died of AIDS about 1995.

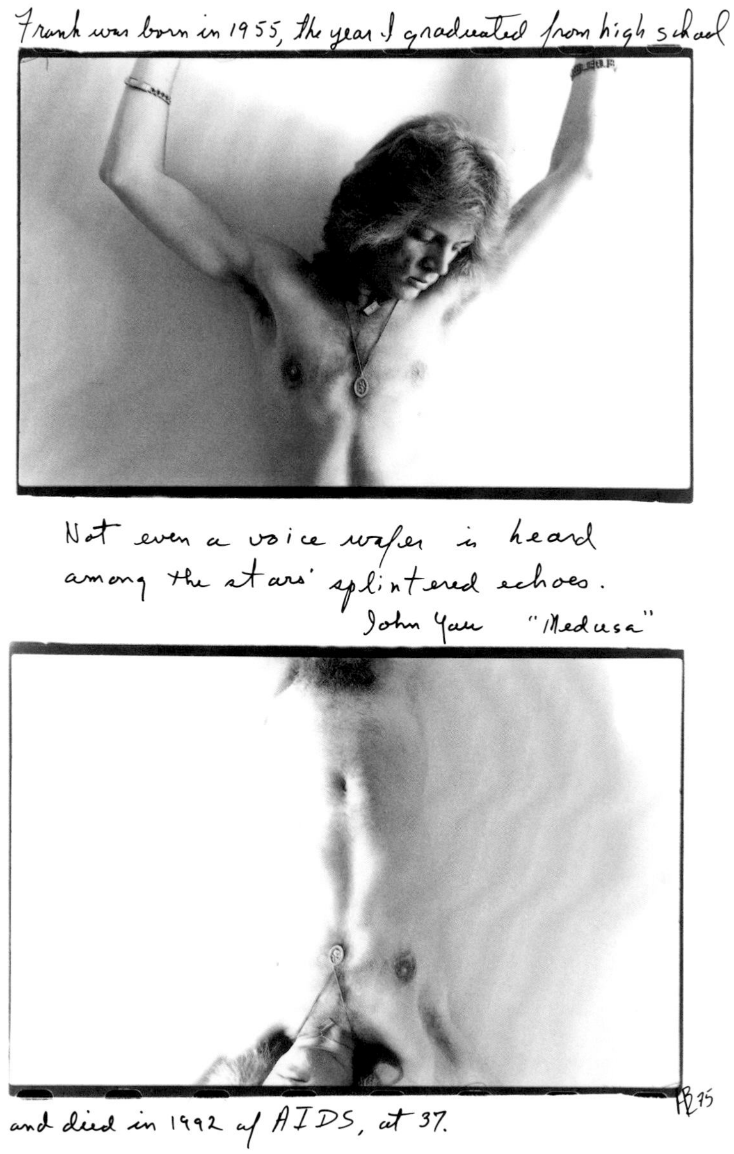

a queer kid's life. This is, in part, what makes the echo of an almost Christ-like crucifixion in Frank's arms and downcast head so poignant. If a hostile environment or hostile city didn't promise to cut Frank down, a hard-edged life would. His heart was caught between sharp pleasures and supposed protections.

The narrative lines that are laid across the surface of this mirrored image appear again as the first line of the second of Grundahl's photos within this collection, "Frank was born in 1955" (II). This is in many ways a denser image. Frank's hair is up in curlers, his cigarette cocked, the expression in his eyes as inscrutable as it is challenging, disbelieving, and enigmatic. The assortment of charms around Frank's neck make explicit an ironic, visual pun of "Frank was born in 1955" (I): that, while Baltimore is known as "Charm City," the charms don't quite protect their wearer from the city or the "difficult night in the Baltimore bars." "Frank was born in 1955" (I) and (II) were both taken in the same year, 1975. The allegorical overtones of the first photo are peeled back in the second. The art of the flowing blond hair of (I) is up in curlers in (II): the art of the first image is crafted by Frank's skill evidenced in the second. Badertscher detects in the underlying story of Frank's fight through the minefield of his family life the significance of his talent as a hairdresser. Though the shrapnel of drugs, violence, and sexual abuse exploded outward against the shell of his inner life, he attempted to craft a new life and art for himself with the help of the tools that he had—stripping and hustling and hairdressing. His intense sexual charisma and persona flare forward in his stare. A deranged admirer of this photo is met with an equally deranged and self-protective flash of eyes.

For me, these photographs do not embody or represent a melancholia, which is caused, at least in part, by the perceived differences between what is and what was. The handwritten narratives that cradle these photos do induce melancholy as they mark unseen births and unwitnessed deaths, but the photos them-

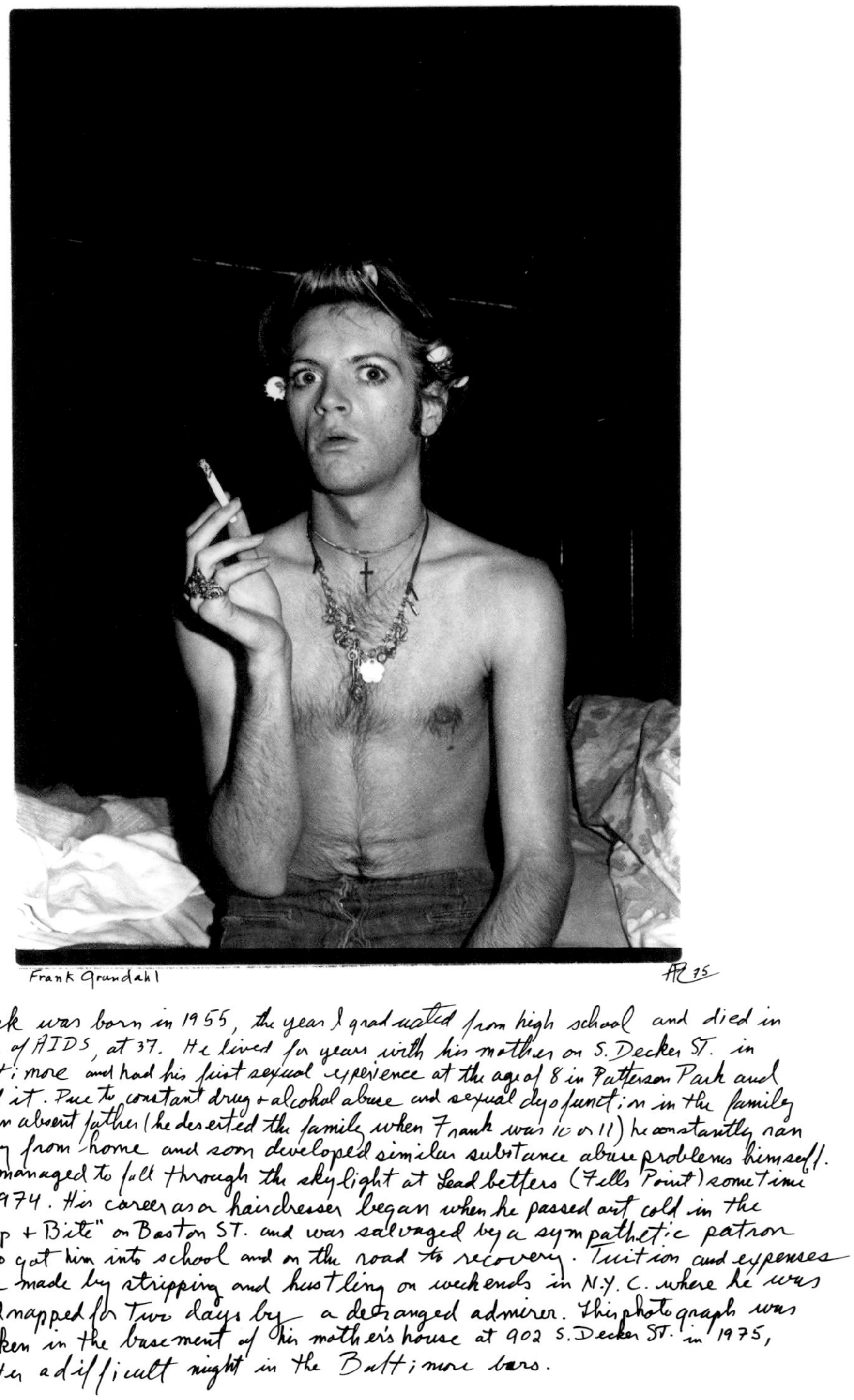

selves aren't melancholic. Although we imagine that we can read the death of these men and women in their eyes, in a stance, in a gesture or glance, I think that this is a lie we tell ourselves, a lie meant to control what we can't, to console ourselves the best that we can. Suffering, pain, despair, pleasure, fury, glee, manic joy, contentment, anxiety, hurt, agony, boredom: emotions and actions are a few of the legible qualities that bubble to the surface of the photograph. Death isn't a quality.

I don't mean to deny melancholy's significance in working through the photographs, however. Melancholy is a fragment of mourning. Mourning is the larger, longer, interpretive process. In the case of Badertscher's work, as with the best of documentary photography, mourning is the labor of struggling with photographic meaning. Mourning gets you from what was to what is.

Perhaps the relationships between mourning and meaning in Badertscher are best brought out by comparison to Duane Michals's haunting work. Michals rocks meaning back and forth across the frames of his photo narratives. Each frame takes a slice out of a story that the viewer is asked to reconstruct. The form itself demands that the reader shift back and forth between photos to make the emotional and semiotic links between images, characters, settings, and handwritten narrative. Badertscher makes comparable though compressed moves. Badertscher collapses writing and image into a single frame: in his most extraordinary distillations, he uses the words of the person he photographed, such as John's in "Amos, Just a few lines to say Hello!"

Taken in 1977, Badertscher's photograph of John is pushed down into the mass of John's letter to Amos from prison. The letter is so extraordinary and detailed, I am at a loss to provide an account of it that would reach into its erotic poignancy, intelligence, not-quite-repressed manic desperation, and small-time hustler instincts for self-protection. As the eyes drag across the photo to complete John's sentences, the viewer is forced into an intimate relationship with John's body and his words, his body to his words. John's gaze is threatening, thrilling, riveting.

The narrative engine of the letter is John's vulnerability in prison: the letter throws up images of a past freedom (cars, girlfriends, fucking with men, major theft) and present peril (the threat of broken bones and broken spirits) to secure Amos's belief that John will survive only with his help. Vulnerability and violence ride the edges of Badertscher's photograph. John cups his cock in his left hand, his body's weight centered on his left leg. His chin slightly down and his eyes focused, John challenges and cruises the viewer simultaneously. He plays out the logic of the letter with breathtaking force.

Melancholy surfaces with the thought that the letter remains unanswered except by our stare. Melancholy, like vertigo, compares here and there. It is the dizzy, stomach-sickening look downward and backward through the letter. By the echo of John's voice from a prison cell, we know what was and what (might have) happened, but there is no present to grasp to steady ourselves. What's left is mourning, the impulse to answer back.

The sometimes accidental, sometimes deliberate fragments of jewelry, hair, clothes, bodies, postures, flair, events in their lives, narrations of their lives: these are the pieces of self that these subjects contribute to the art of the photo. Some images teeter between a modernist, clean-edged, almost sculptural presentation and a blurred romantic one. Both modes are used at different times in different ways to convey a sense of what was and is real, a sense of the documentary. Images embedded in narrative also convey that these people lived both pleasure-filled and difficult lives. The artistic objects, image and text, photo and graphic, are as unsentimental as they are immediate, erotic, and pleasurable. Each photo/graph is a distillation of the rich tones, tastes, and textures of a Baltimore community. Badertscher's work exclaims: they not only lived but continue to live.

This is the present tense of queer photography.
This is the present tense of photographic space.

We are here.
This is now.
These are our lives.

A Note on the Photographer and the City of Baltimore

It is common to call people who do not have a formal artistic education "self-taught," but there is something about the term that elides the complex routes by which a person learns a craft. Amos Badertscher did not have an arts education in photography. When he took up his camera, he also took the advice of a fellow teacher at a Baltimore prep school where he taught mathematics: get close to your subject. The camera can absorb a subject's personality just as much as it can take on the photographer's. The processes through which Badertscher learned the technical skills of his art were crafted by his attention to the people he photographed; each helped to guide the other.

Perhaps it is ironic that a math teacher should move so deftly away from controlled patterns and forms. The manner by which he learned to photograph shifted the aesthetic weight from a heavy-handed, formalistic style to what Badertscher characterizes as rapid-fire, unstructured sessions. An extraordinary amount of concentration on the interplay of photographer and subject within the session is needed, however. Badertscher was given the time to work through the problems posed by this style when he inherited some money from his parents in the mid-seventies.

Importantly, his style evolved in concert with the people he photographed: some were his friends, many

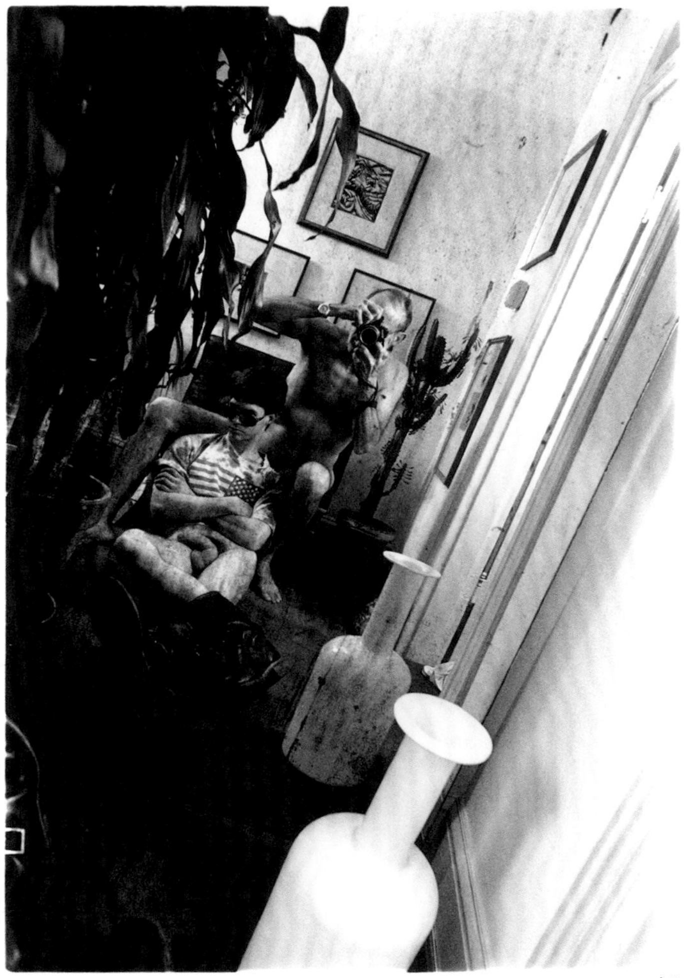

Self Portrait with Billy HB '94

were Baltimore drag queens and hustlers, youths on the prowl for loose cash and drugs. Badertscher believes that it is easy to moralize about the complexities of the lives of people who live on a hard edge. To his eyes, the political (and, indeed, moral) failings of the gay and lesbian community are located in an attitude that wants to play the complexities of drugs, familial abuse, disease, and sexual power against an attitude of social respectability. Political expediency is bought with the blood of people who are written off as alienated by their own "perversions."

Certainly, AIDS, drugs, sexual, and social puritanism have ripped through the communities that these photographs document. Though this book is not a history of the queer communities of Baltimore, that history cannot be written without the people that Badertscher's work captures. Nor can these people and photos be properly understood without a reference to Baltimore itself. In many ways, the emptying out of the industrial Northeast left Baltimore to rust. With respect to its economic history, Baltimore shares the fate of many East Coast port cities. As with all large American cities, race governed—and in many ways continues to govern—the flow of people from sidewalk to sidewalk, neighborhood to neighborhood. Baltimore's racist past has not been fully put behind it. Despite real and lasting progress, racial tensions within the city, and within the gay community, still polarize people and resources.

In concert with the macrodynamics of race and class, sexuality carves out its own sections of the city. Guilford and Roland Park, large neighborhoods to the north and east of Johns Hopkins University, are known for their wealthy and white populations. Just north of Guilford, sections of Towson are settled by middle-class African American families. Baltimore has poor white neighborhoods, just as it has poor black neighborhoods. Downtown Baltimore, especially in the Mount Vernon area, is less homogenous in its racial makeup, however. This heterogeneity might be due to the large number of queers that live along St. Paul Street and Charles Street and their adjacent streets. The center of the city's clubs, bars, groceries, specialty shops, hairdressers, bookshops, and restaurants are all gay and lesbian friendly, if not queer owned and operated. The large number of gays and lesbians who live within the city's borders makes them an important voting block and political force: queers are courted by mayors and city council members alike.

But queer sexuality easily mobilizes powerful homophobic political alliances across race and class lines, within the city. For instance, in the early 1990s, a number of conservative African American churches joined with conservative Jewish groups and Christian Coalition types to defeat Baltimore's domestic partnership bill in the city council. The support of African American civil rights organizations, reform Jewish synagogues, and sympathetic Christian organizations could not put out the "Moral" Right's raging vitriol and fear. A "prayer ring" formed outside the city council building after the defeat of the domestic partnership bill. Once again, queers were forced outside the civic circle by the bigotries of religious bonding.

The politics of AIDS writes large the religious, class, racial, and sexual antagonisms as they are fought within Baltimore's civic and social arenas. Predominantly white and gay male AIDS service organizations fight for every political dollar that they can get to help Baltimore's large People With AIDS population. African American AIDS organizations not only compete for that money but also have to fight the silences and hostilities around homosexuality and AIDS in the African American community, as well as racism and hostility in its interactions with a white queer community. A large population of intravenous drug users within Baltimore and Baltimore County comprises both blacks and whites, but they often feel alienated by queer health organizations, African American AIDS organizations, and the numerous church ministries that have stepped into the void of government assistance. There is cooperation as well as antagonism, but the pressures of attempting to manage AIDS within one's own body at times leave people with little energy to manage the problems within the body politic.

It is striking and sobering that, to one degree or another, every one of these important and helpful organizations takes a moralistic stance on the people of *Baltimore Portraits.* Whether that stance is against real or perceived patterns of gay male sexual contacts ("promiscuity" is the most common red-flag term), the exchange of sex for money (as opposed to all of the other things for which sex is exchanged—say, love—and not often safely), or any same-sex sexual contact at all (churches like to call it "Homosexuality" with a capital H and sweep all "perversions" under its rug), its moralism serves to confirm the respectability and right-thinkingness of the one who casts judgment. Again let me say that if Badertscher's photographs do not offer a particular moral perspective, it is a testament to his photographic technique and philosophical commitment to the complexity and worth of queer lives.

Definitions

I would like to jot down a few notes about my use of the term "documentary photography" and the word "queer." By definition, documentary photography makes claims on what is real. Early confrontations with photography as a medium tended to treat the photograph more or less as the passive representation of an unmediated "reality." Ethnography, to name only one of myriad disciplines that picked up photography as just such a "descriptive" tool, found itself caught in epistemological tar traps as it used the photographic image to gesture transparently toward the reality of its subjects/objects. At times, these disciplinary catalogs were met with (at worst) derision and (at best) skepticism by the people who were subjects of and subjected to their categories. The histories of the native peoples of North America, for instance, cannot be written without an extended discussion of the engagements between (white) photographers and (Other) Native Americans. Modern definitions that acknowledge the problems tend to shift the emphasis to a distinction between the "staged" and "not staged" in the attempt to define some core characteristic of "documentary."

Clearly, queer photography troubles the distinction between staged and not staged: the people who inhabit a queer documentary project conspicuously acknowledge the malleability of categories that in other contexts might be "fixed." Masculinity, femininity, and sexual self-presentation are only the most immediate examples of categories that, in contexts outside the queer arts, tend to be taken at what can only ironically be called "face value." Both Nan Goldin and Robert Mapplethorpe are, by this definition, "queer photographers," a term that takes in sexuality but doesn't slice off areas as "gay" and "straight" based on the sexual identity of the photographer. At best, perhaps, what documentary photography "documents" in these cases are people as icons of their lived lives—moments, spots, gestures, looks, instances of the transient and ephemeral. Claims to the documentary must, above all, acknowledge the role within the artistic process of those who are documented. Obviously, this means rejecting an auteur theory of photographic creation. The photographer, though important, is not the only one who determines meaning within the photograph.

"Queer" parallels this definition closely. No fag or dyke ever leaves grade school without having heard the term "queer." The first time I heard it was in the context of a game: "smear the queer." The boy with the football was the queer and the rest of the boys tackled him, thus the smear. Eve Kosofsky Sedgwick, a scholar who has helped redefine the term queer, analyzes the semantic leverage afforded by third person enunciations of any term of contempt: you are, she is, he is. Each of these declarative sentences makes a claim on another's existence in order to give the speaker power over the one who is spoken against. You are a fag. She is a dyke. He is a queer. Sexual minorities have absorbed the vicious momentum of these hurled accusations, made them into a proud moniker and embedded them in a new anthem. "We're here! We're queer! Get used to it!" The change in voice makes a distinction in style, makes it clear that we won't live in fear. We are living our desires and differences in pride. We speak in the first person: I am, we are!

End Note

1. For a discussion of "queer," as well as my take on documentary photography, see the section "Definitions" on p. 10 of this essay.

As I've indicated in my definition of "queer," I owe much to Eve Kosofsky Sedgwick's work, especially the introduction to *Novel Gazing: Queer Readings in Fiction* (Durham: Duke University Press, 1997). Her analyses of the performative force of first-person and third-person articulations occur in the opening pages of *Epistemology of the Closet* (Berkeley: University of California Press, 1990) and *Tendencies* (Durham: Duke University Press, 1992). Also important in the formulation of this introduction's terms and reading strategies is Jonathan Goldberg's essay on the photography and sexuality of Laura Gilpin, "Photographic Relations: Laura Gilpin, Willa Cather," *American Literature* 70, no. 1 (March 1998): 63–95. Though Gilpin's work is in another aesthetic universe than Badertscher's, Goldberg's attention to and elucidation of what he calls the "affective links" between her art and her life are an object lesson in the importance of paying attention to the stories behind and within the photographic image. Stephen Oldenberg Barber's "Lip-Reading: Woolf's Secret Encounters," in *Novel Gazing*, pp. 401–443, evokes many of the fierce aesthetics that I found in Badertscher's portrait "Todd had too many personalities."

My affection and gratitude goes to Ed Suarez for putting his private collection of photographs at my disposal. Ed's extensive photographic library and substantial knowledge of photography were invaluable to this project. Much affection to Liz Kelleher for her enthusiasm and support. Finally, much respect and many thanks to Amos Badertscher. He spent hours talking to me about the photos and sharing with me his own private edge of Baltimore.

This essay is for Alan Stephens.

BALTIMORE Portraits

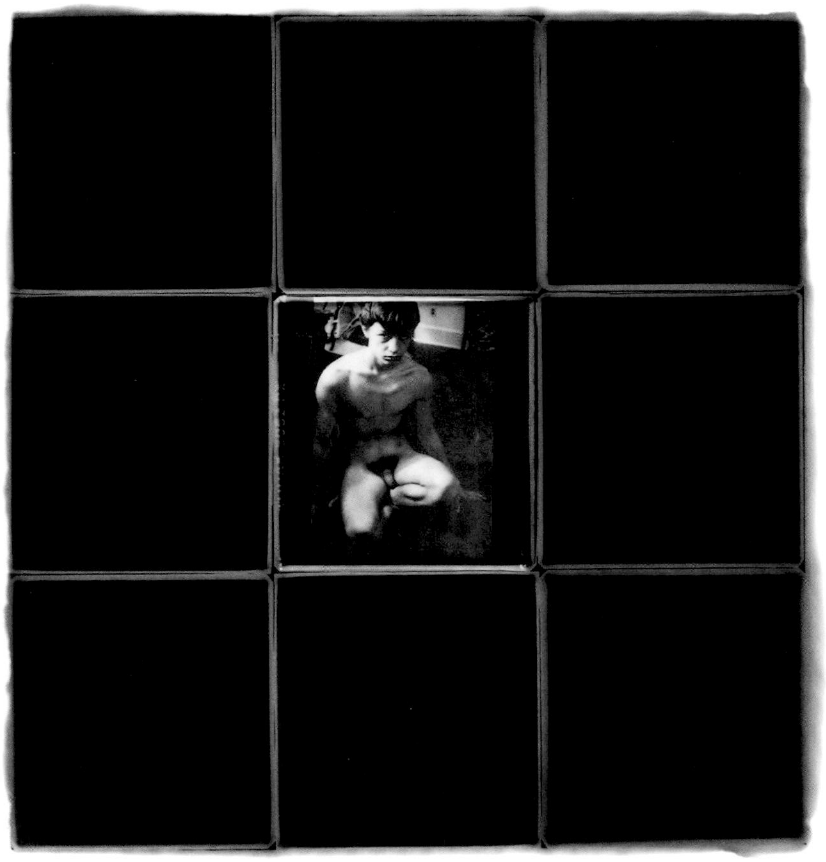

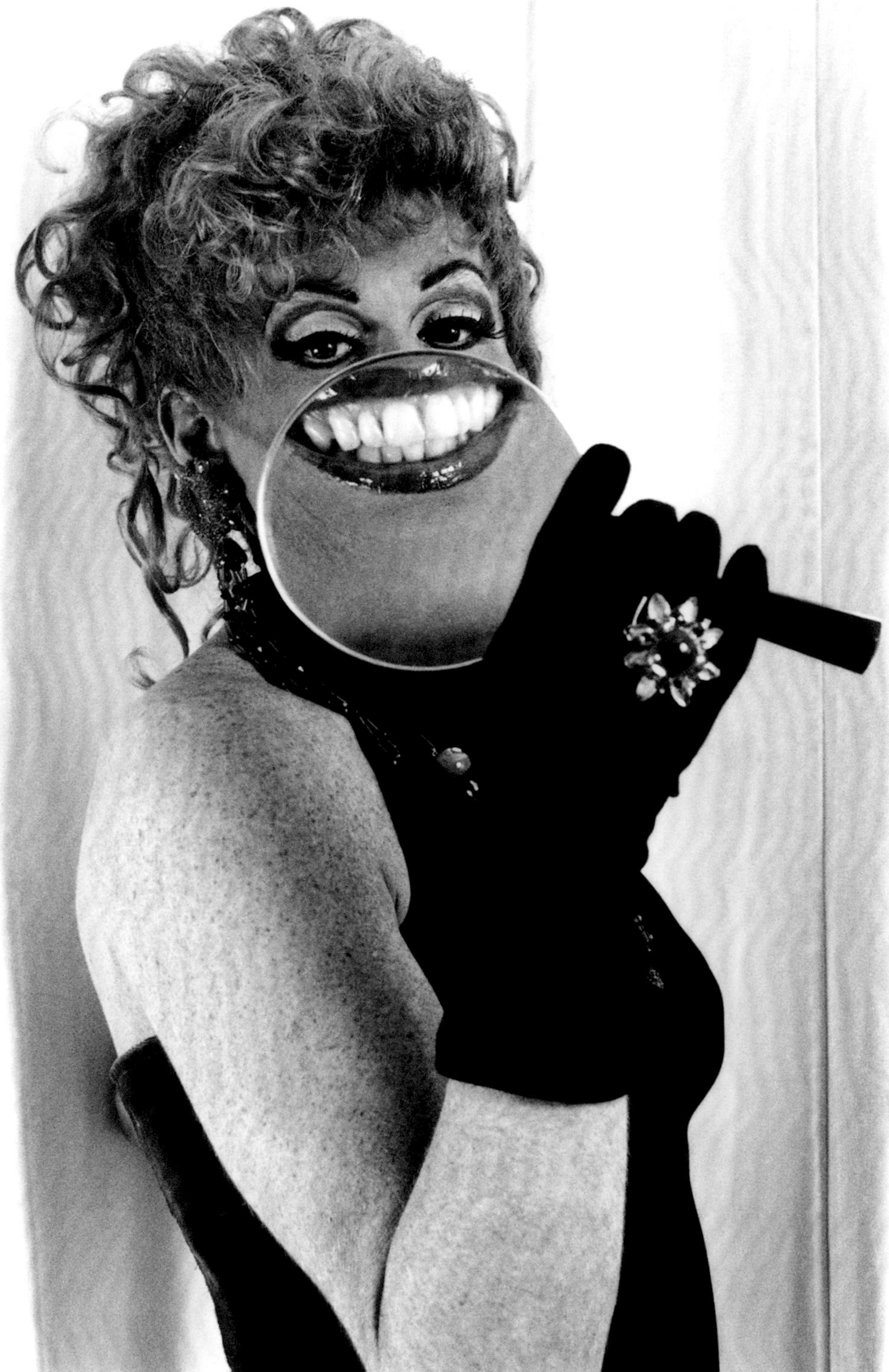

Miss Jennings: died Jan. 1996

AB '94

She was born with a fist in creation's asshole + little tolerance for creatures of the planet Earth.

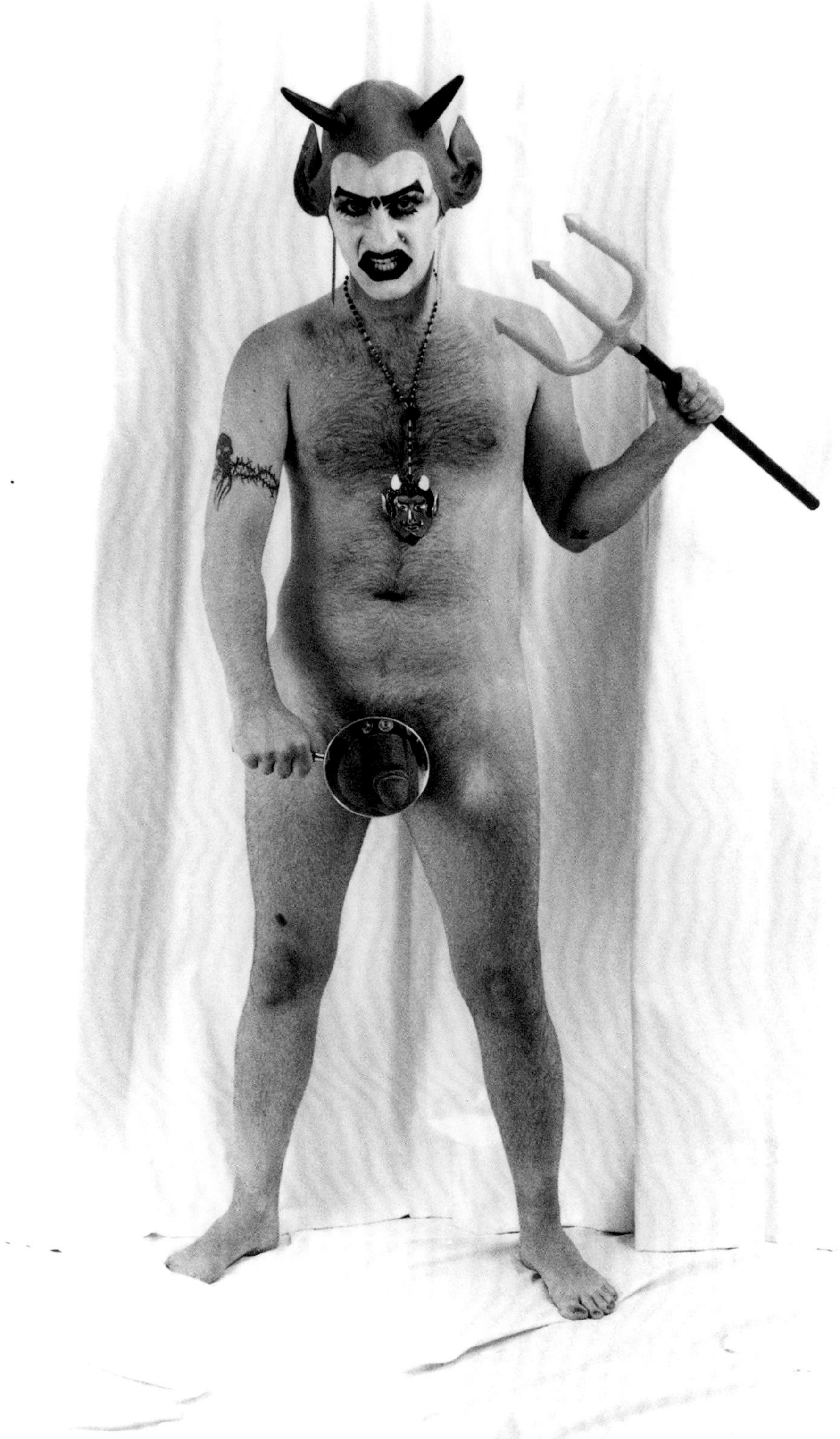

Hermaphroditee

AC '93

Early on Jeffrey pulled open the emergency door of life + jumped in. If anything could shock this broad it is not of human design.

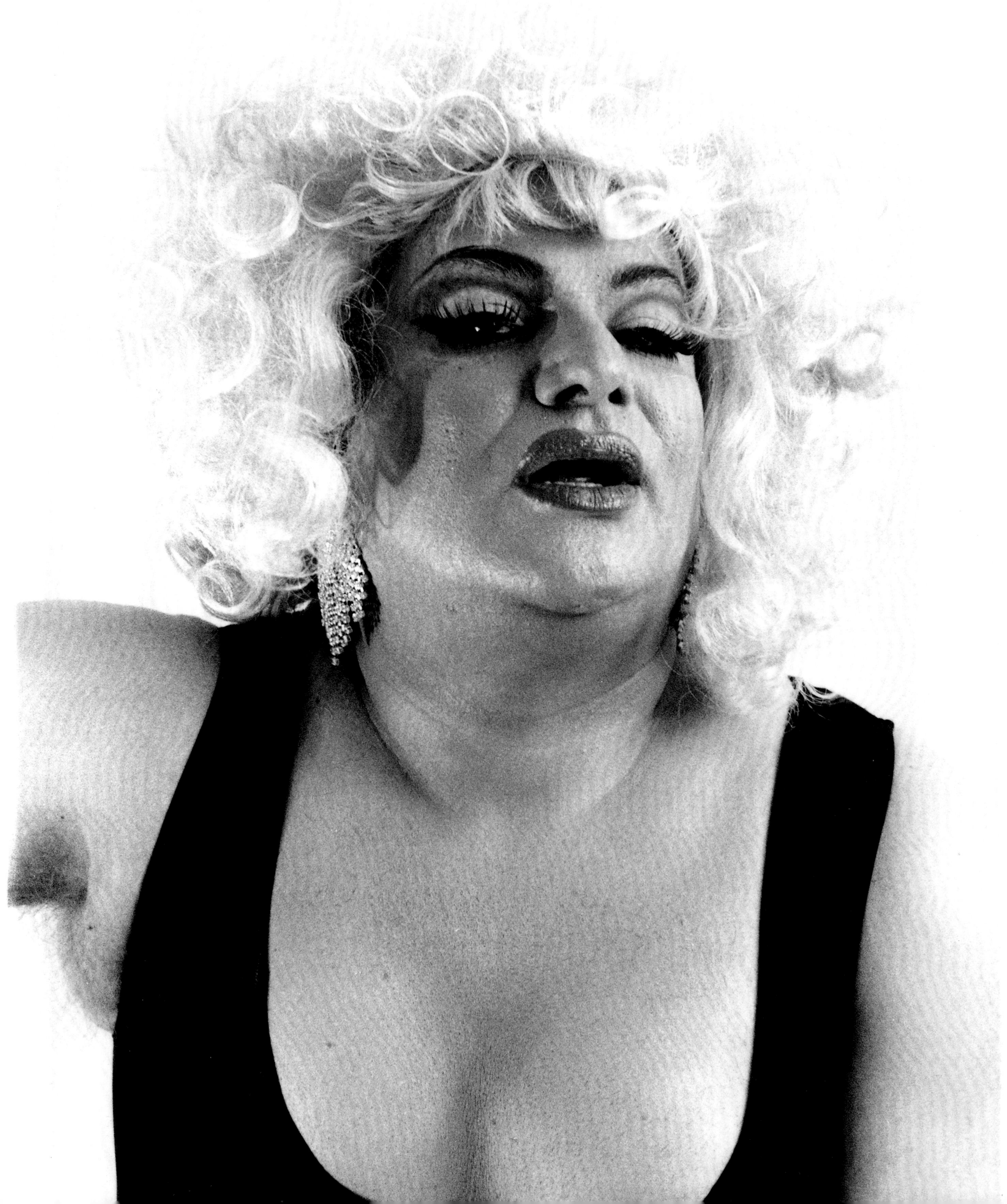

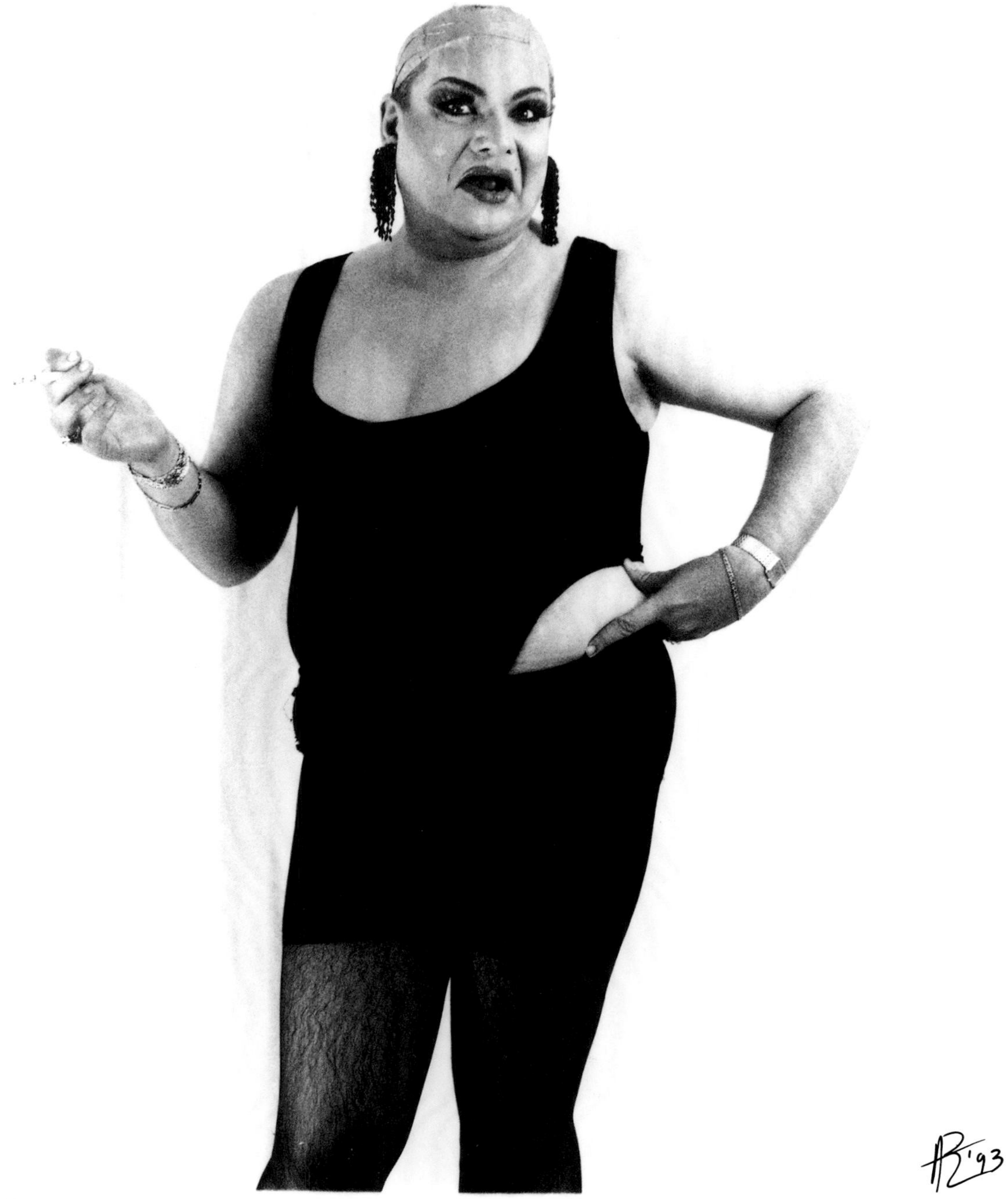

Miss Jamie: beauty engineer xxx-traordinaire

Her mother made the marriage of the century and left her bags of uncut diamonds. At 16 she had tons of blond hair and was sent all over the world because people were in love with her. At one time she did a hair fashion show fa the Walters Art gallery in Baltimore and did the fall + spring line fa Givenchy (Paris). The remainder of the jewels, art and original furniture not found in her apartment on the thirteenth floor of Hopkins House are safely displayed in her other houses.

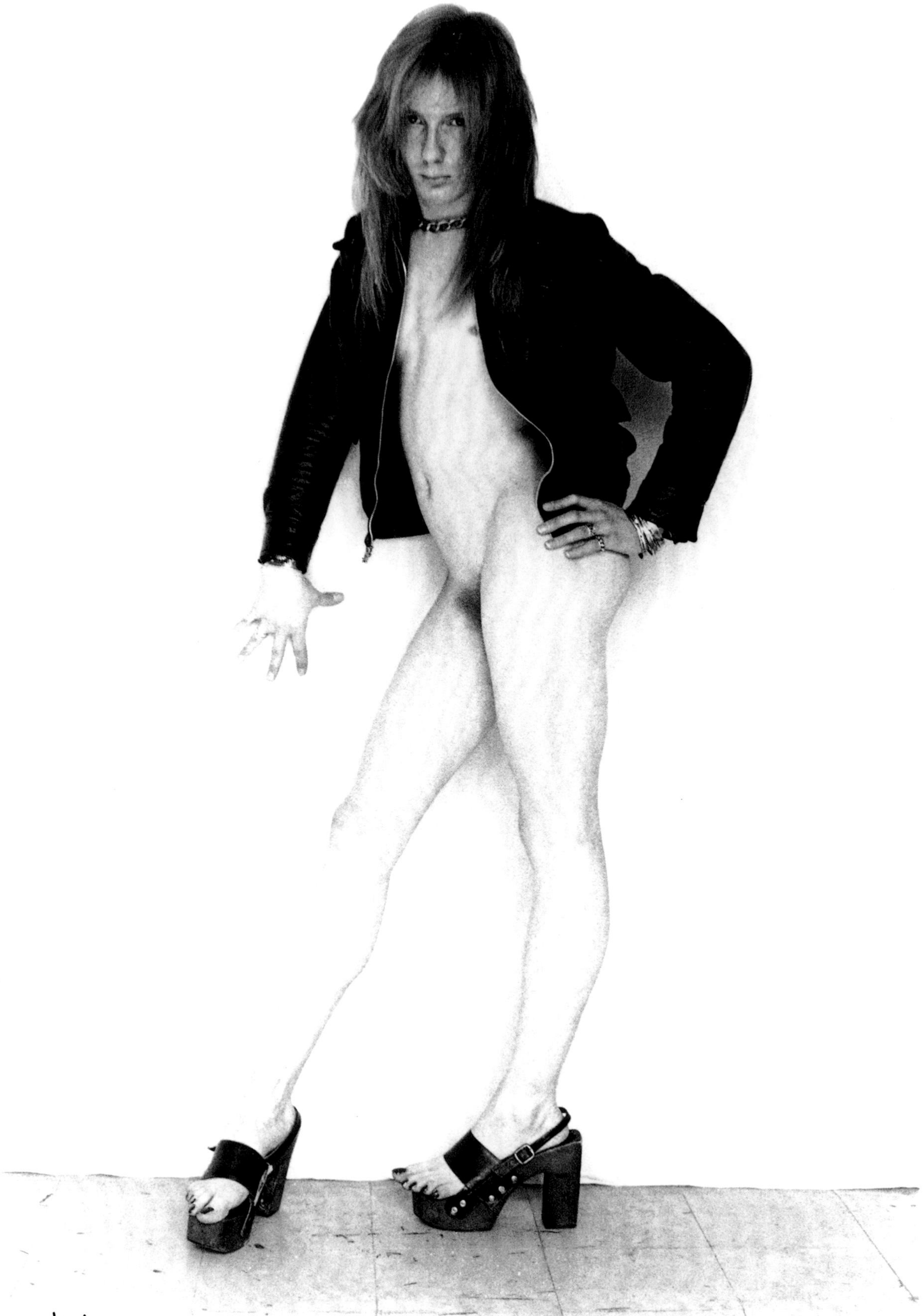

Kris Krixer

AR '78

a rocker in the late seventies.

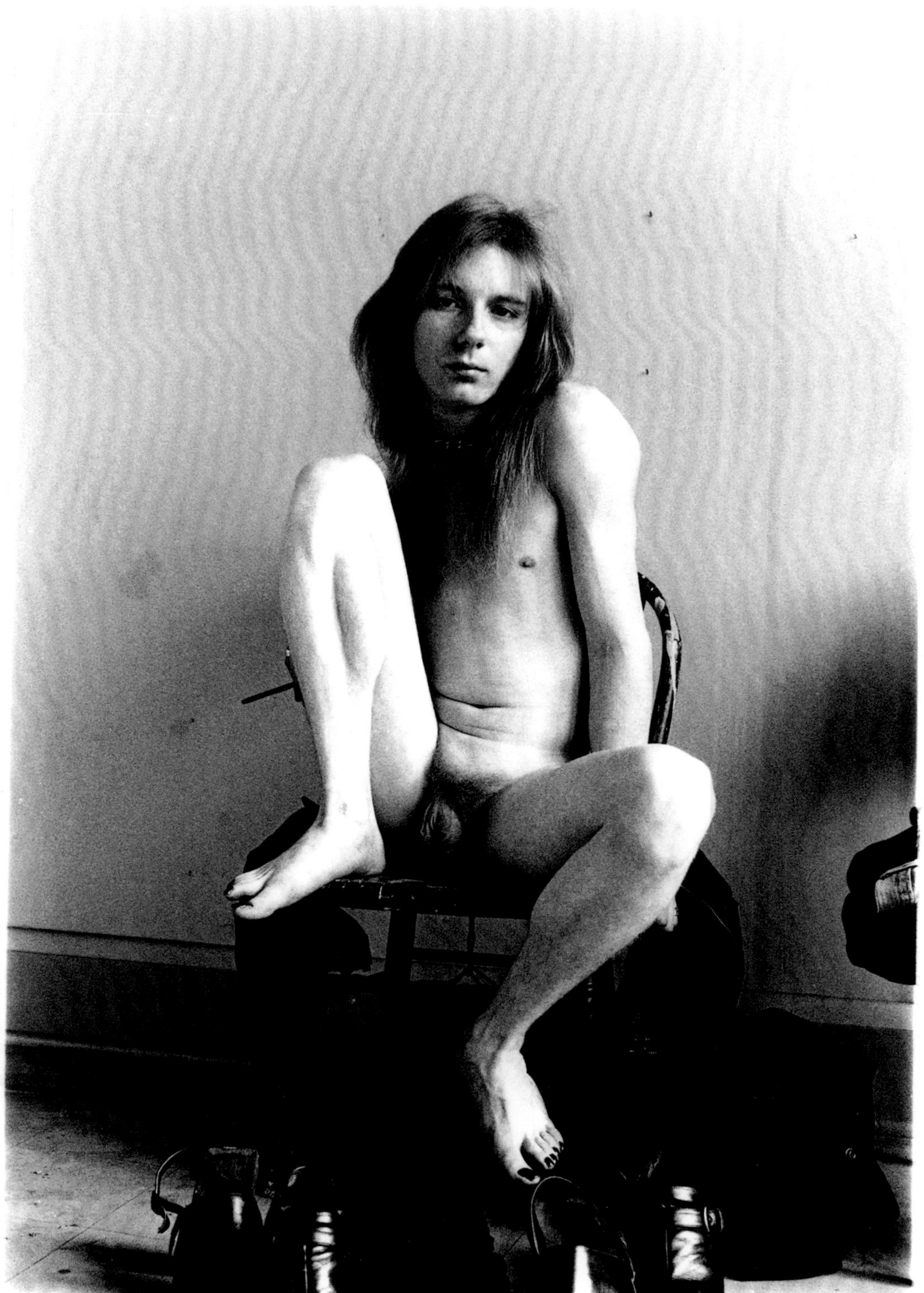

Kris Krixer

AB 78

A rocker in the late seventies with an extensive groupie following.

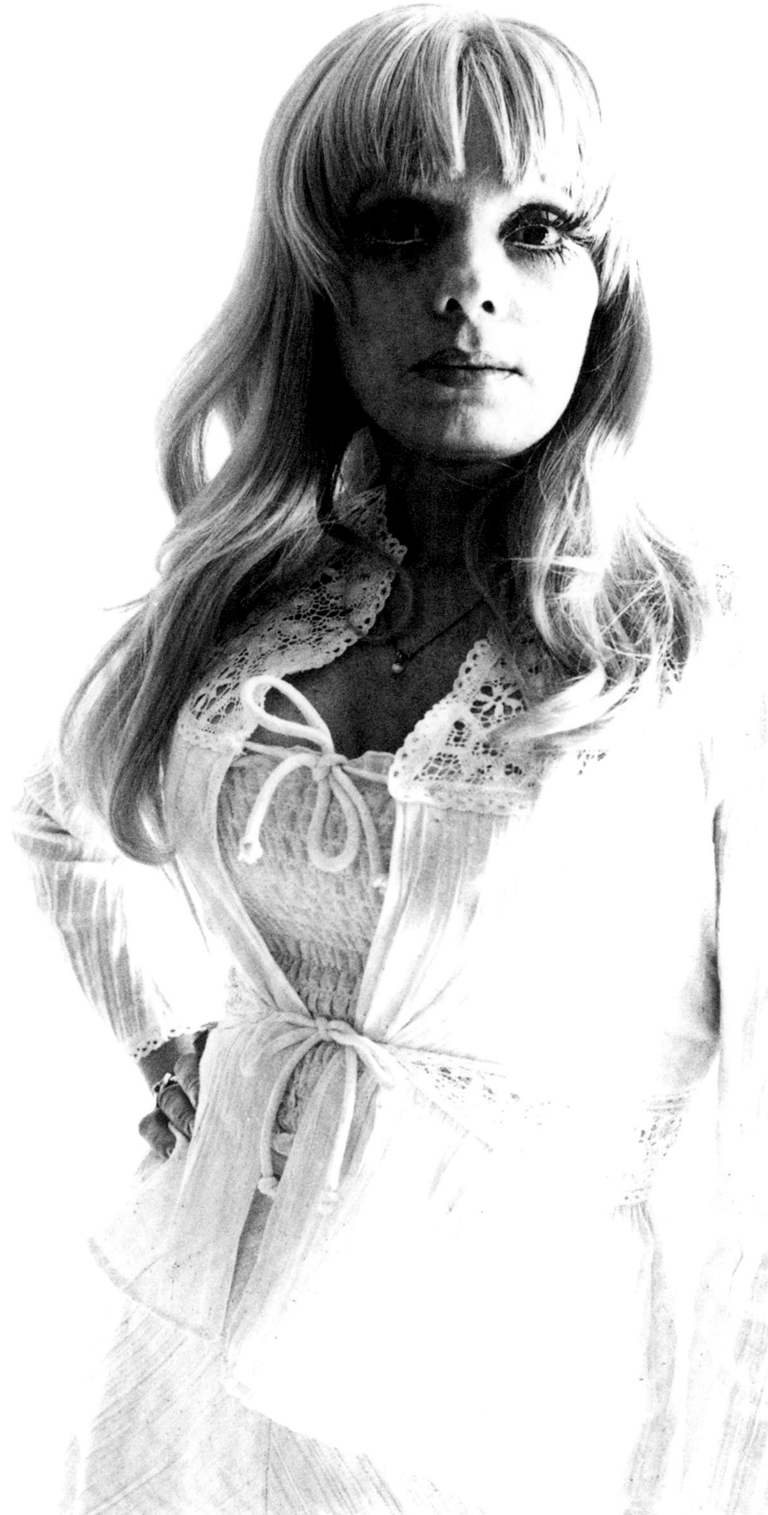

'76

Sandy was this very sweet person who frequented gay bars and was somehow part of the night life of the 70's. She lived with her mother, liked tight dresses and wanted very large breasts. The silicone injections led to epidermal dysfunction and cancer. She died in the late 70's. She could be seen at the bar in Leon's almost to the very end.

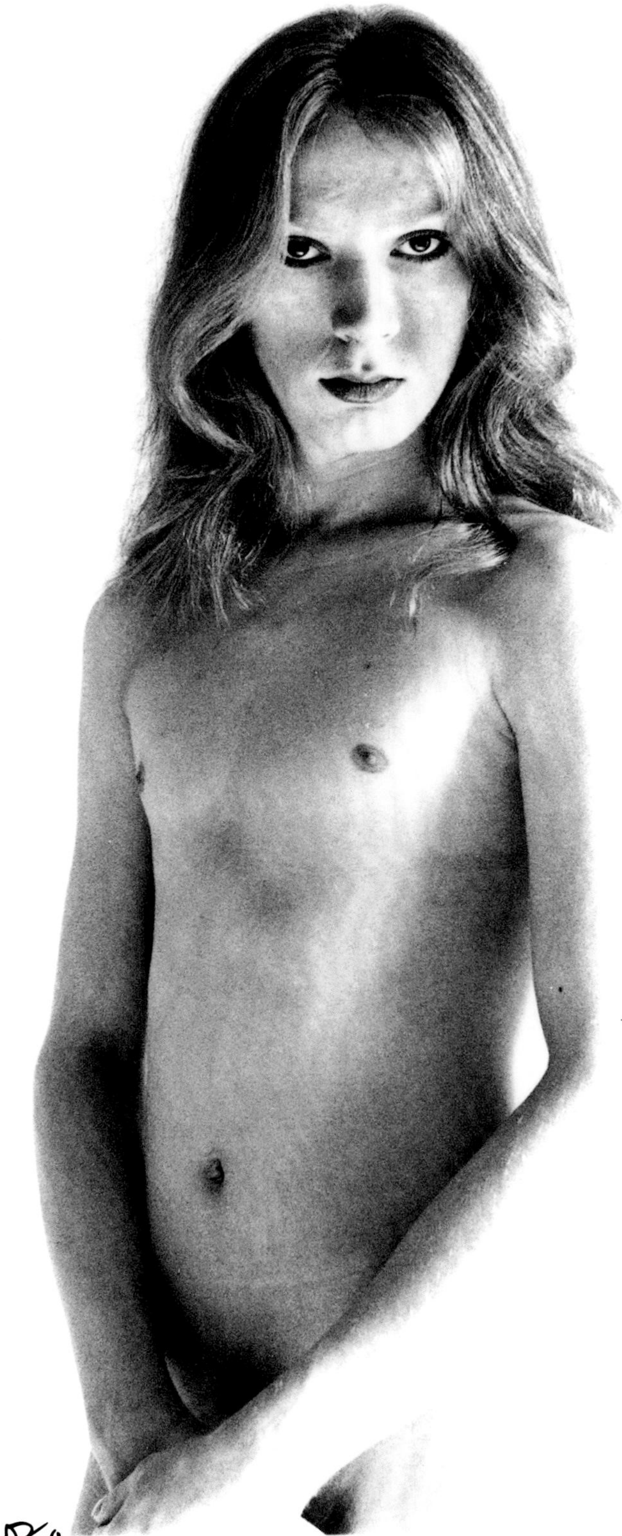

Sandy the mild prostitute – at eighteen. Her haunt was Eastern avenue supplying services all her life to men who needed people like Sandy. Initially, a sexually abused child from Armistead Gardens in Baltimore City, uneducated, her only indulgences were a few beers, fun with her friends and later on in life, a little witchcraft. For this she earned a few years in prison for prostitution. Her last years were lived with drag queen Mary on Monument ST. and she died in September of 1993 of AIDS at age 32. Her real name: Steve Helmick.

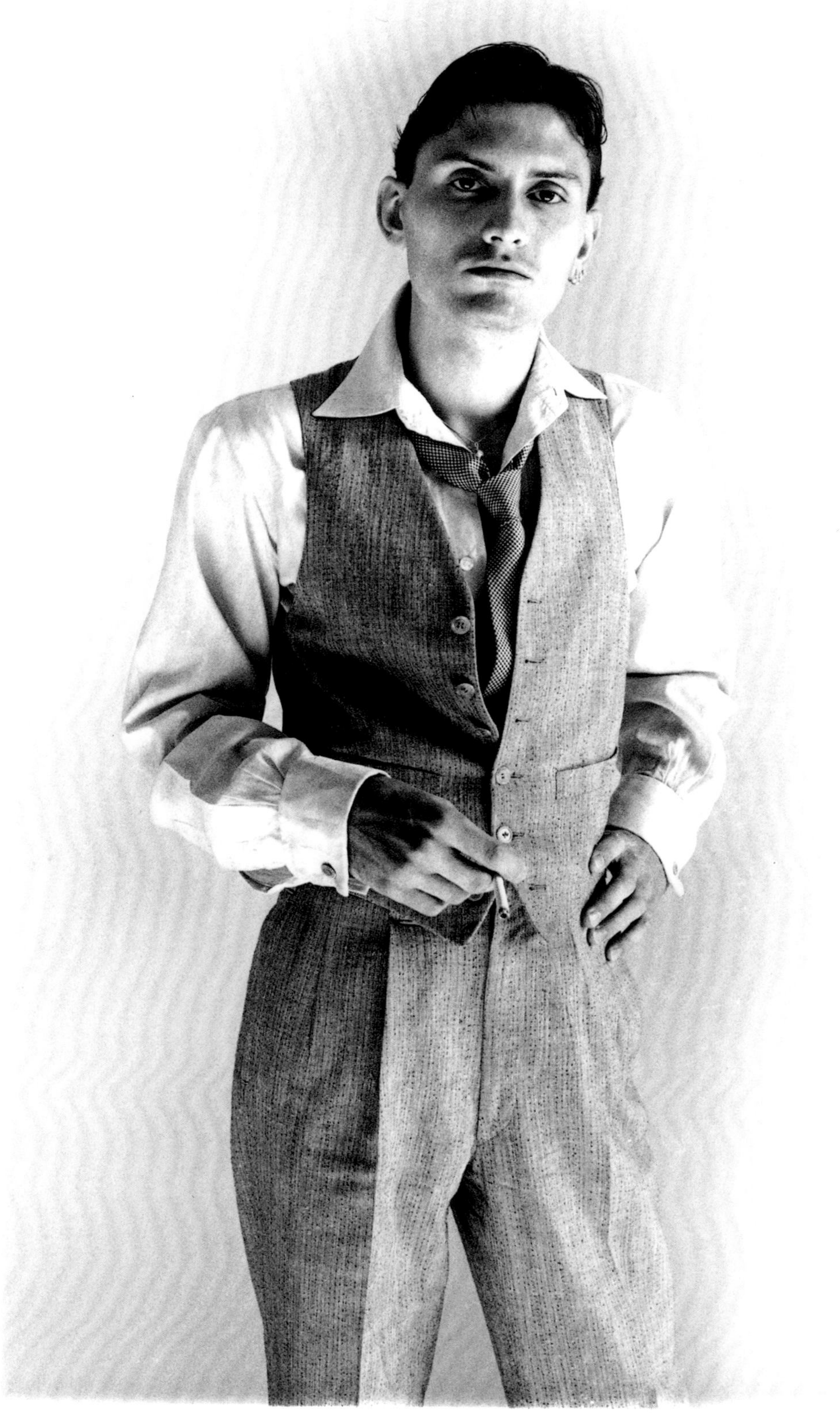

AR.76

The talented and charismatic Baron von Huppert (a.k.a. Keith, Uncle Keith, Uncle K, von): a onetime Iranian hostage, author of an unpublished monograph on putty knives, last and only director of the SoNo Galleries at 1730 Maryland Ave, Baltimore, enfant terrible xxx-traordinaire. The Baron's penchant for writing bad checks, southern gin and later on more advanced stimulants (depressants) led inevitably to a psychic denouement and actual confinement in the summer of 1993. This photograph, taken in 1976, hints vaguely at the Baron's quixotic charm. He was shot to death in Aug. of 1995 by two sixteen year olds.

The Baron von Huppert and Mark became lovers in 1978 when Mark was 18 yrs. old. The Baron older. It was a furious and painfull relationship, one the Baron never really got over. Mark was a young punk. And bright. He wore black and said "smarmy" and "scuzzy".

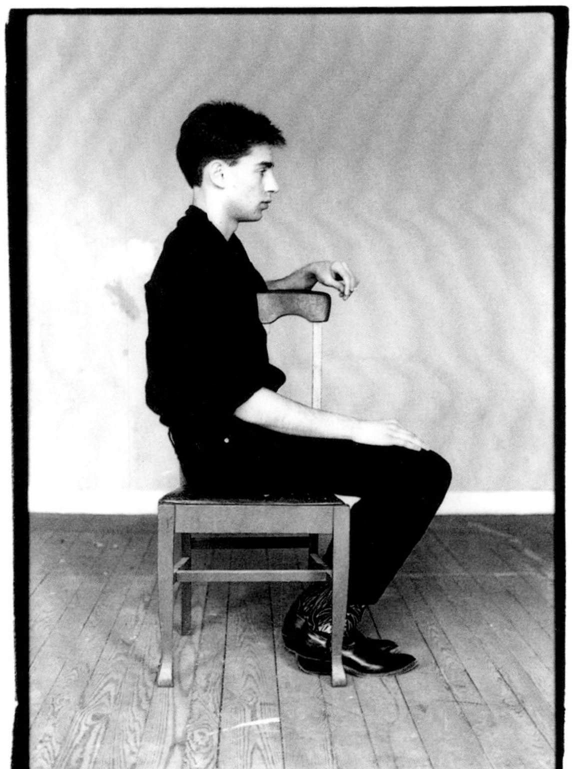

Mark Dumais

AR '78

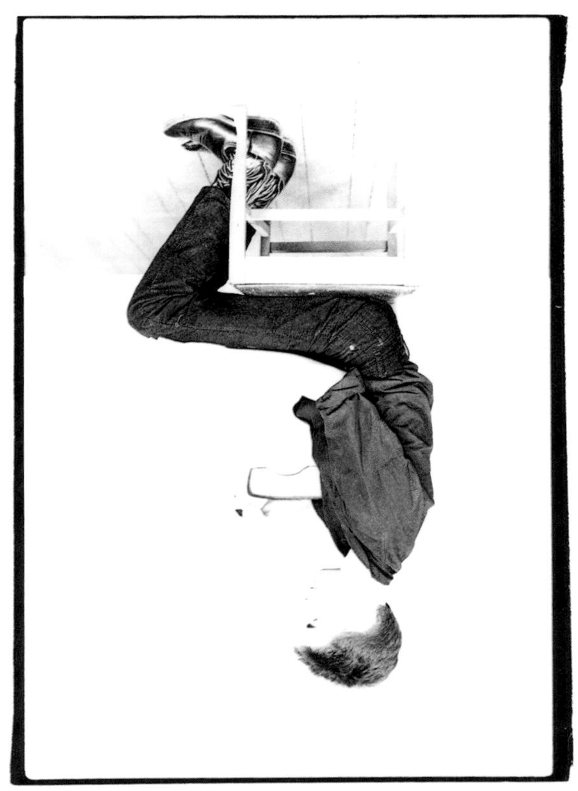

He wanted to be a rock star. In three years they seperated—went their seperate ways. Mark went to N.Y.C. and eventually to London. He made some recordings that prabably still survive. He died of AIDS in 1992, at 32 years.

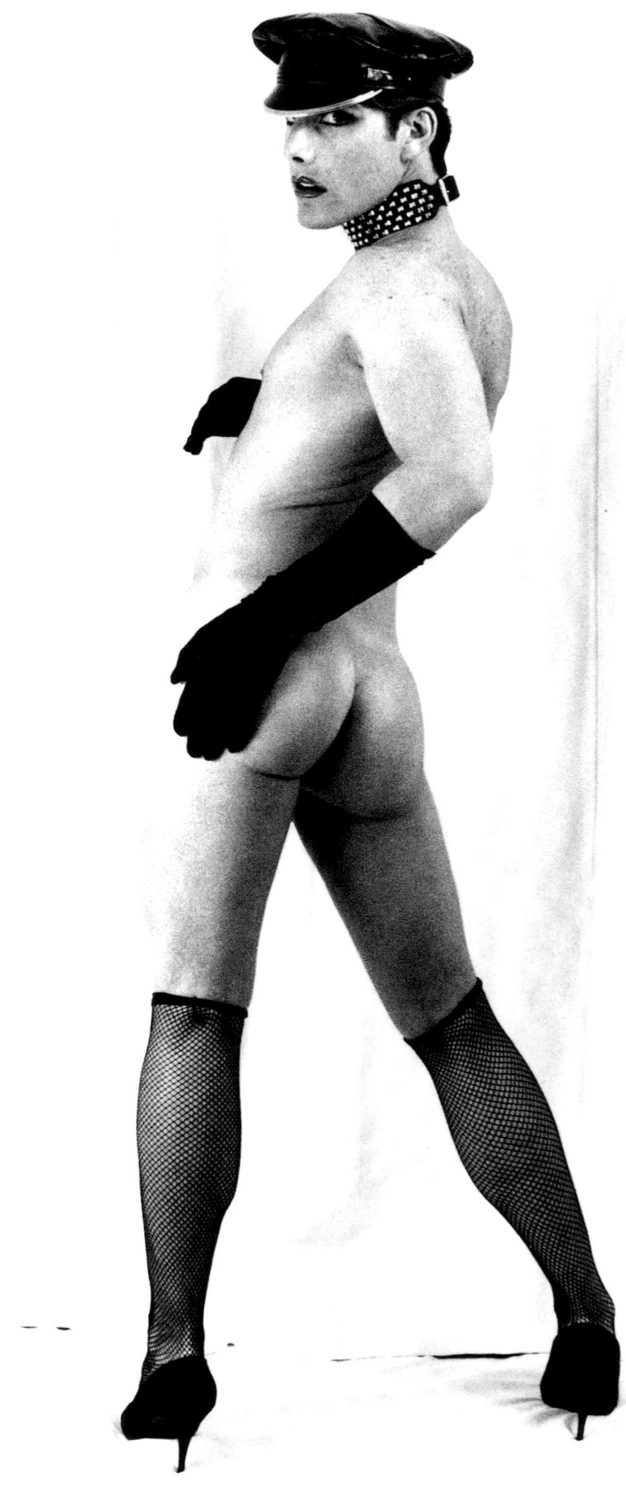

AB '93

Miss Gregory as Wonderwoman

This is a lady you'd better think twice about inviting into your parlour or bedroom.

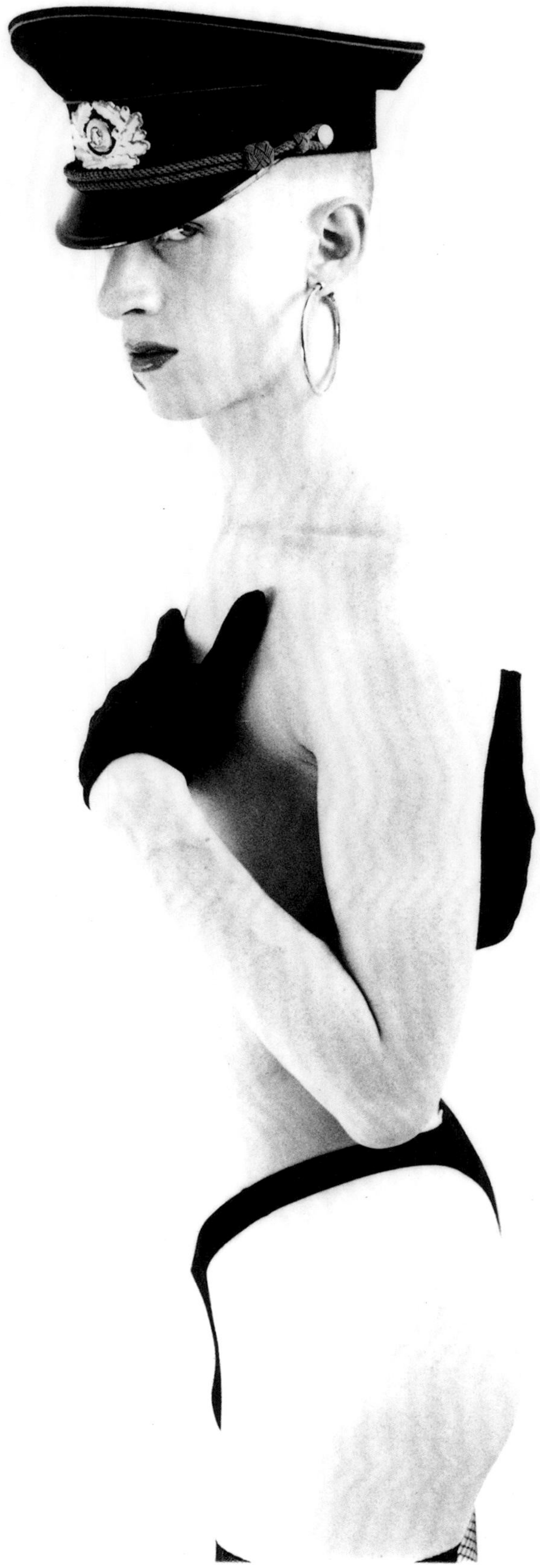

Frankie '92

The Dauphin is captured by the Court Photographer as he emerges from the Royal Bedchamber for a night in the Capital.

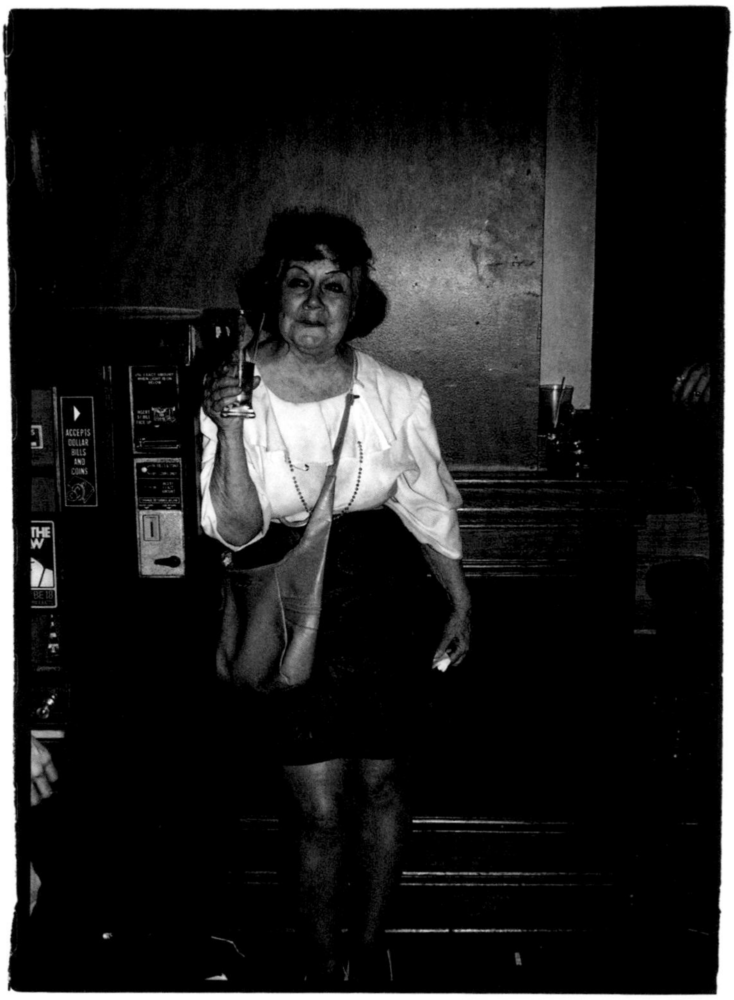

This is Baby Jane. She visits the gay bars on Charles Street on an erratic schedule. This is by the door of Central Station, in May. Sometimes she's quiet, sometimes not. Sometimes drunk. Patrons buy her beers and chat. She likes very much to watch men.

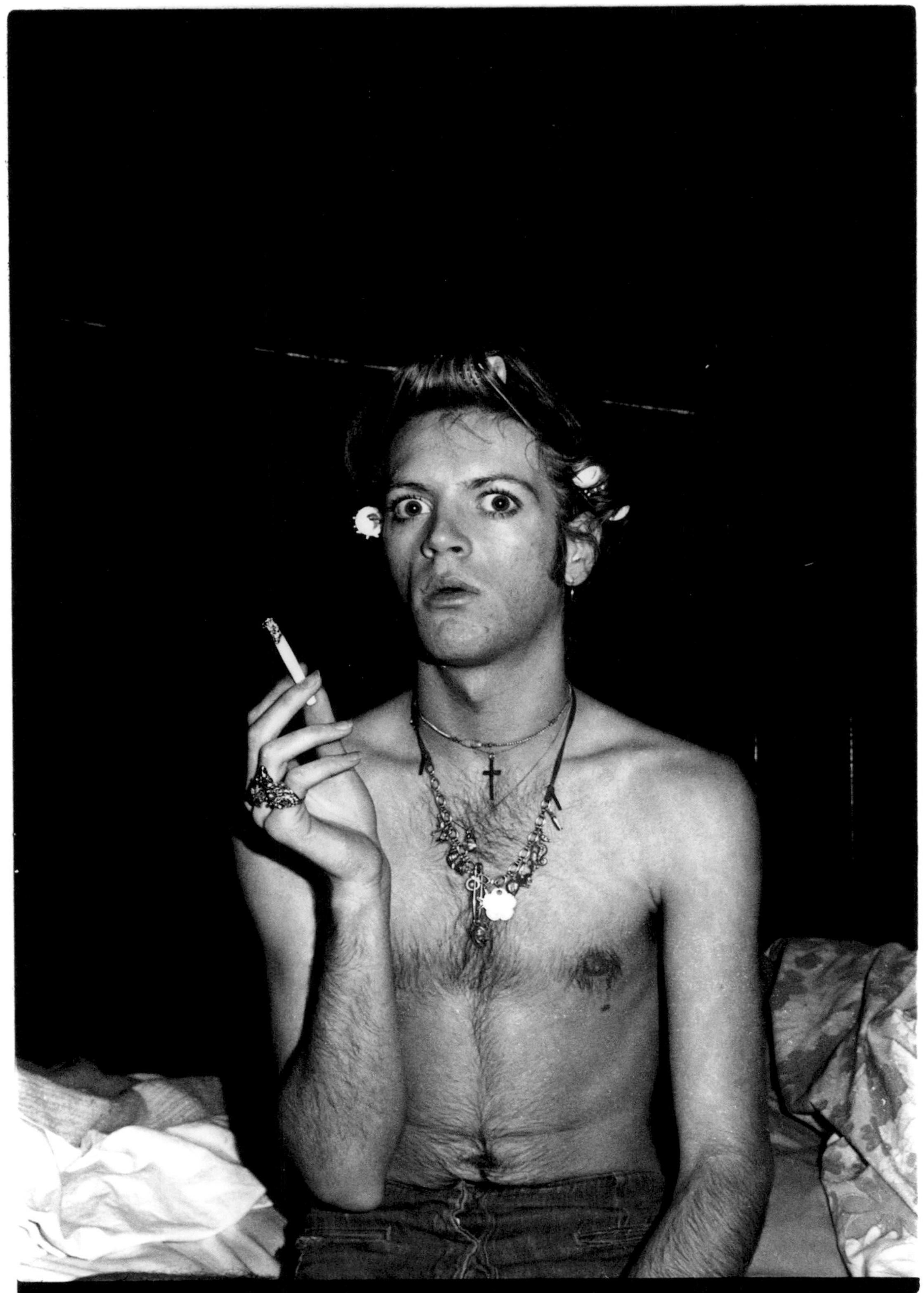

Frank Grandahl AC 75

Frank was born in 1955, the year I graduated from high school and died in 1992 of AIDS, at 37. He lived for years with his mother on S. Decker ST. in Baltimore and had his first sexual experience at the age of 8 in Patterson Park and liked it. Due to constant drug + alcohol abuse and sexual dysfunction in the family and an absent father (he deserted the family when Frank was 10 or 11) he constantly ran away from home and soon developed similar substance abuse problems himself!. He managed to fall through the skylight at Leadbetters (Fells Point) sometime in 1974. His career as a hairdresser began when he passed out cold in the "Sip + Bite" on Boston ST. and was salvaged by a sympathetic patron who got him into school and on the road to recovery. Tuition and expenses were made by stripping and hustling on weekends in N.Y.C. where he was kidnapped for Two days by a deranged admirer. This photograph was taken in the basement of his mother's house at 902 S. Decker ST. in 1975, after a difficult night in the Baltimore bars.

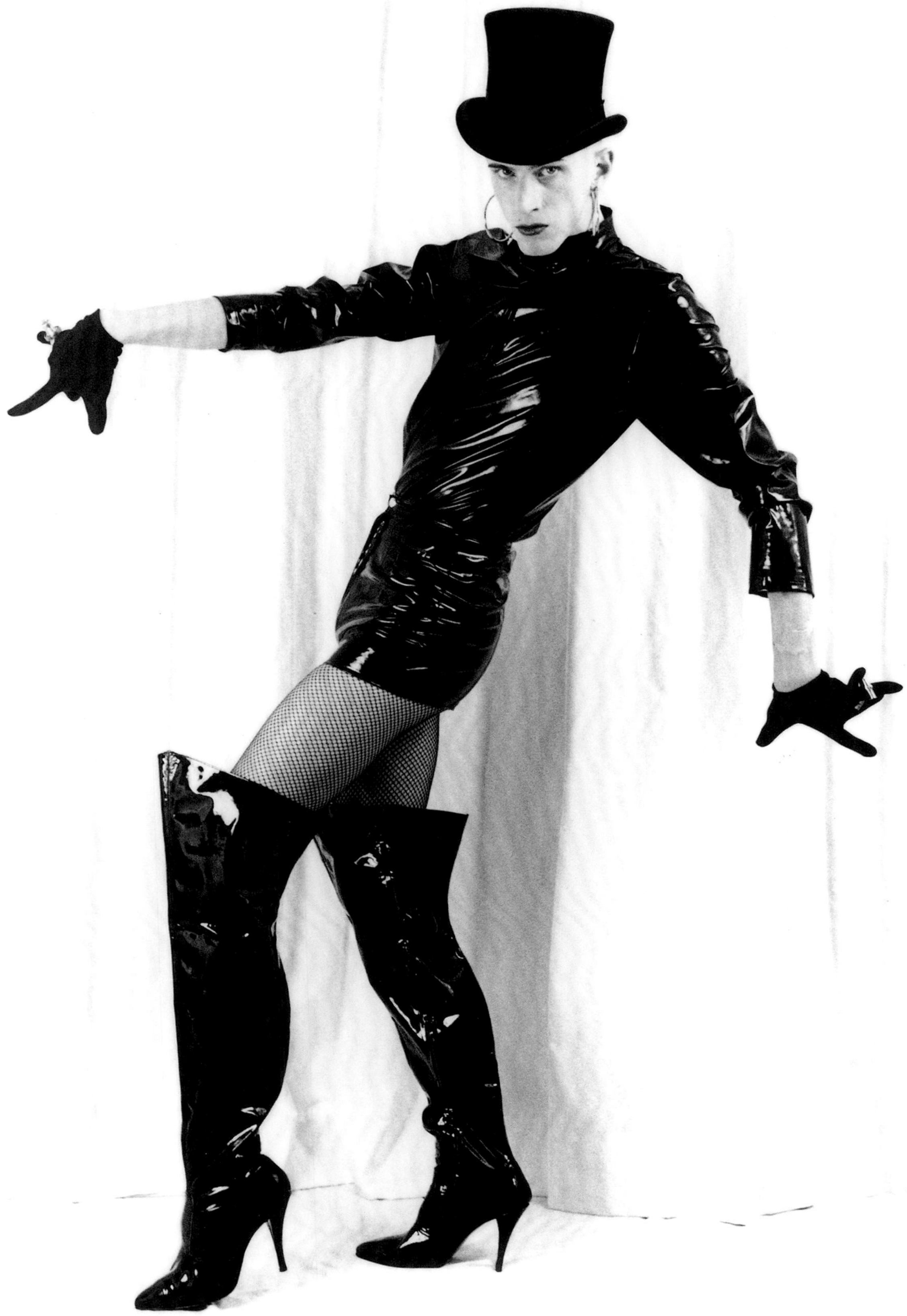

Frankie '92

The Dauphin graces the lens of the Court Photographer.

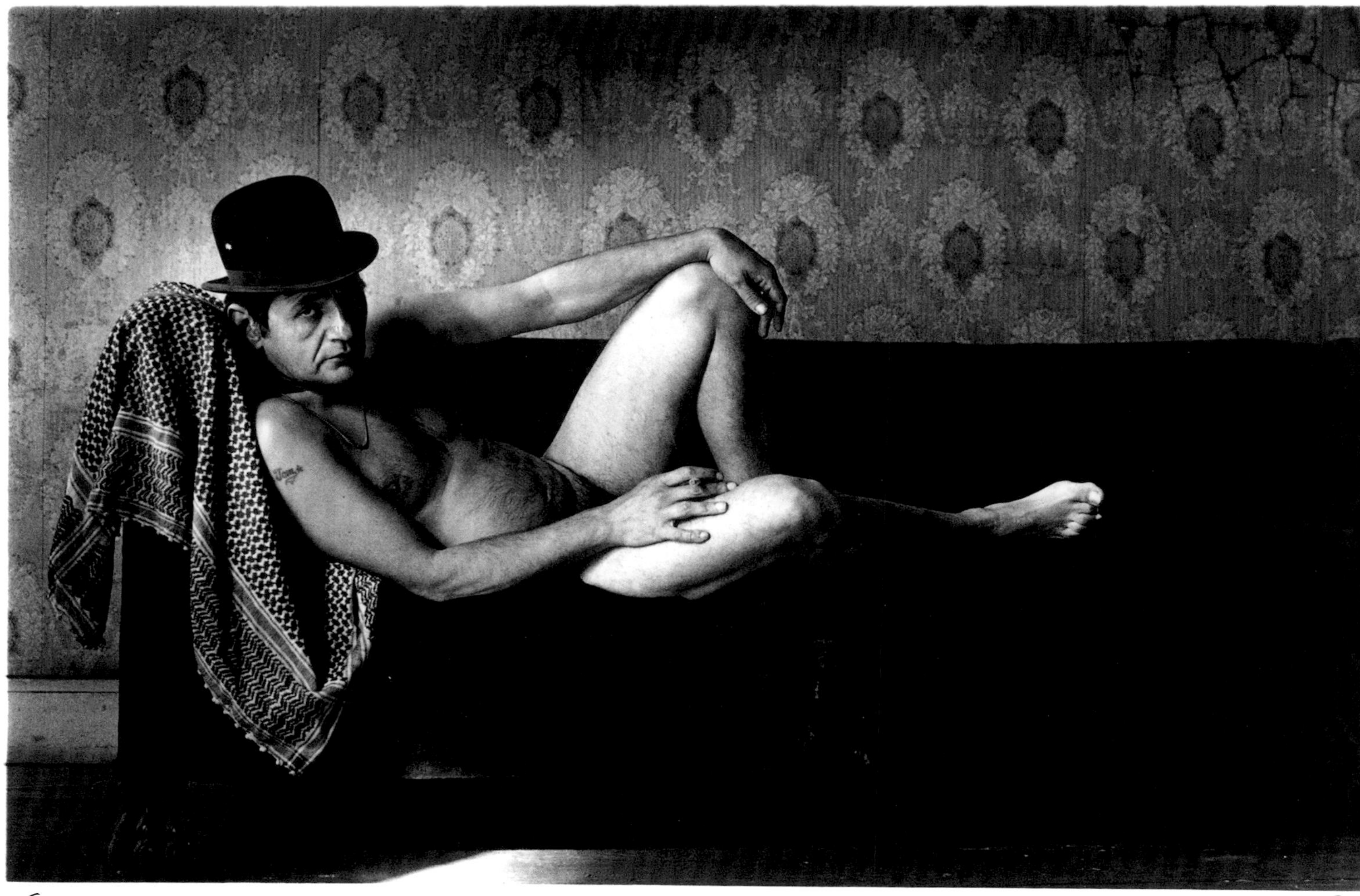

Elliott ✡ [initials] '76

Antique dealer

This is certainly one of the true Baltimore crazies. For years he owned a successful Baltimore antique shop on South Charles St. and managed to maintain a relationship with the Baron von & zu Huppert as his mind increasingly made those detours familiar to the inspired paranoid. He dropped dead of a heart attack in the later 80's unencumbered by conventional moorings.

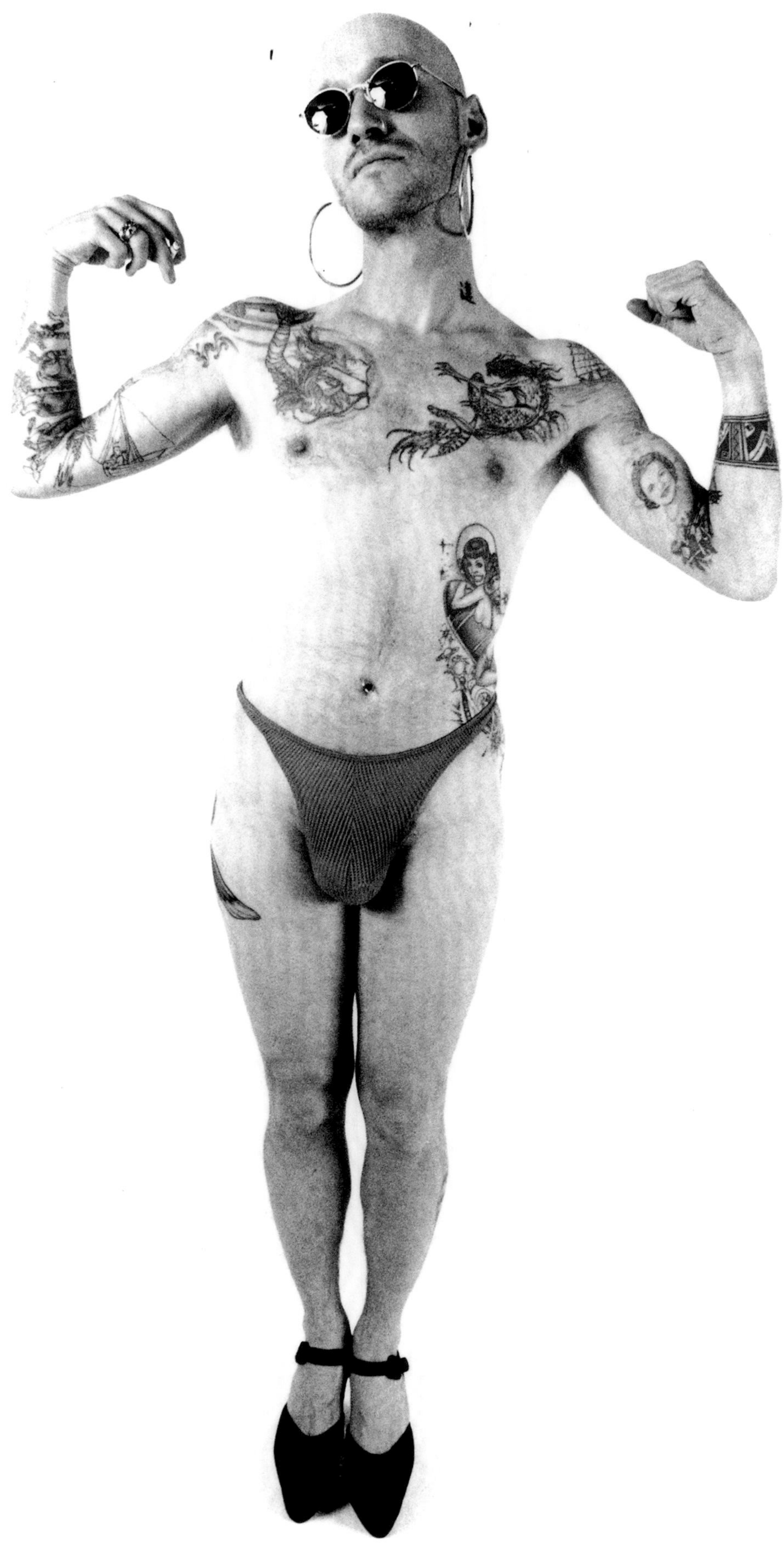

Rick Wilson: Mistress Q

Gay Skin Donor

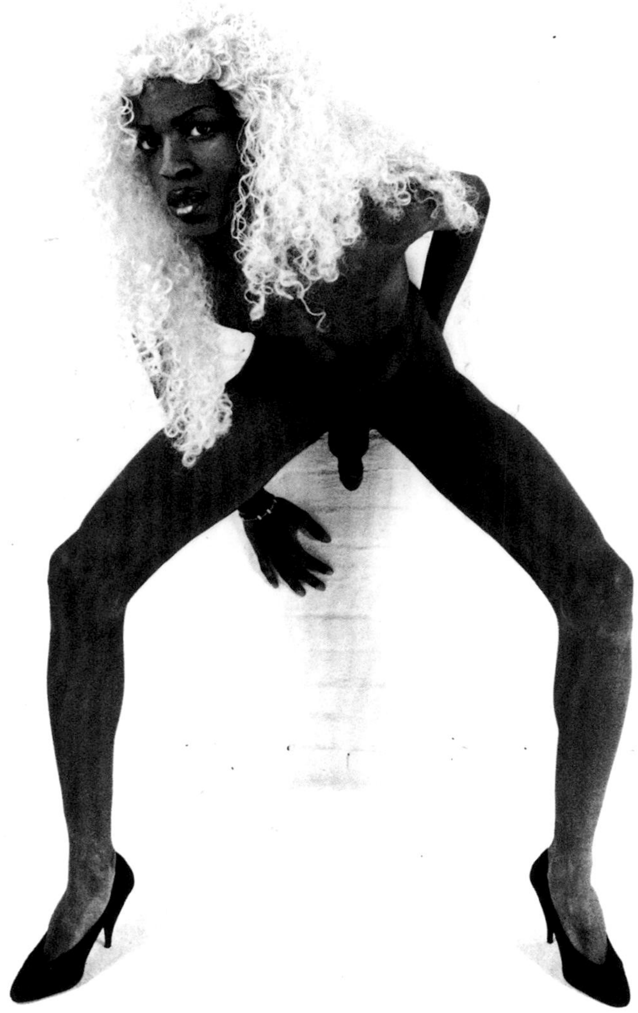

Ramsey

'93

A reformed Jehovah's Witness after witnessing Jehovah.

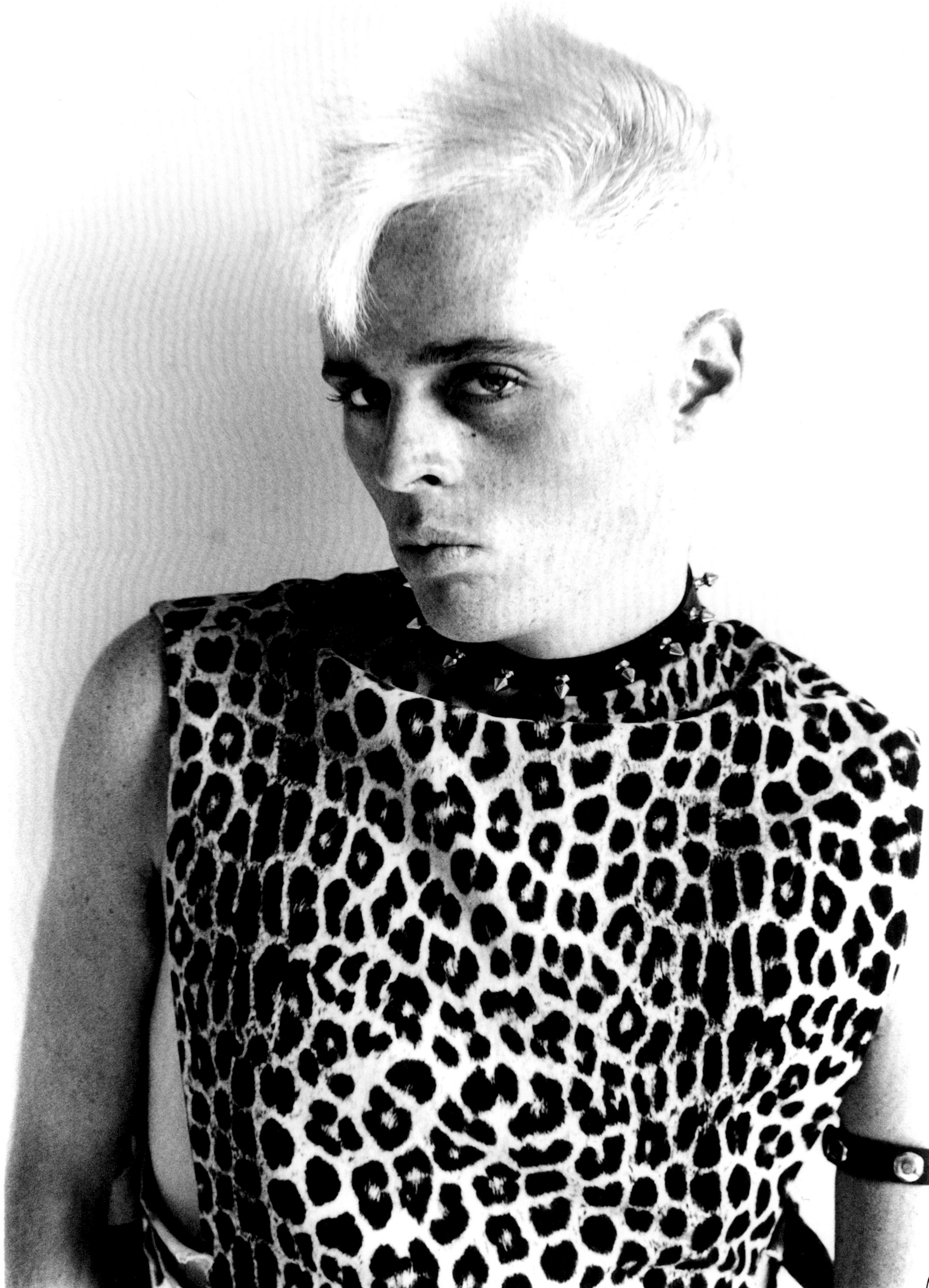

AB '82

George D. Stewart III – Jennings

She was born with a fist in creation's asshole + little tolerance for creatures of the planet Earth. A rare hair stylist with a claw-hammer personality. Sex toys, pink poodles, diva presence. Sample, earthlings, at your risk.

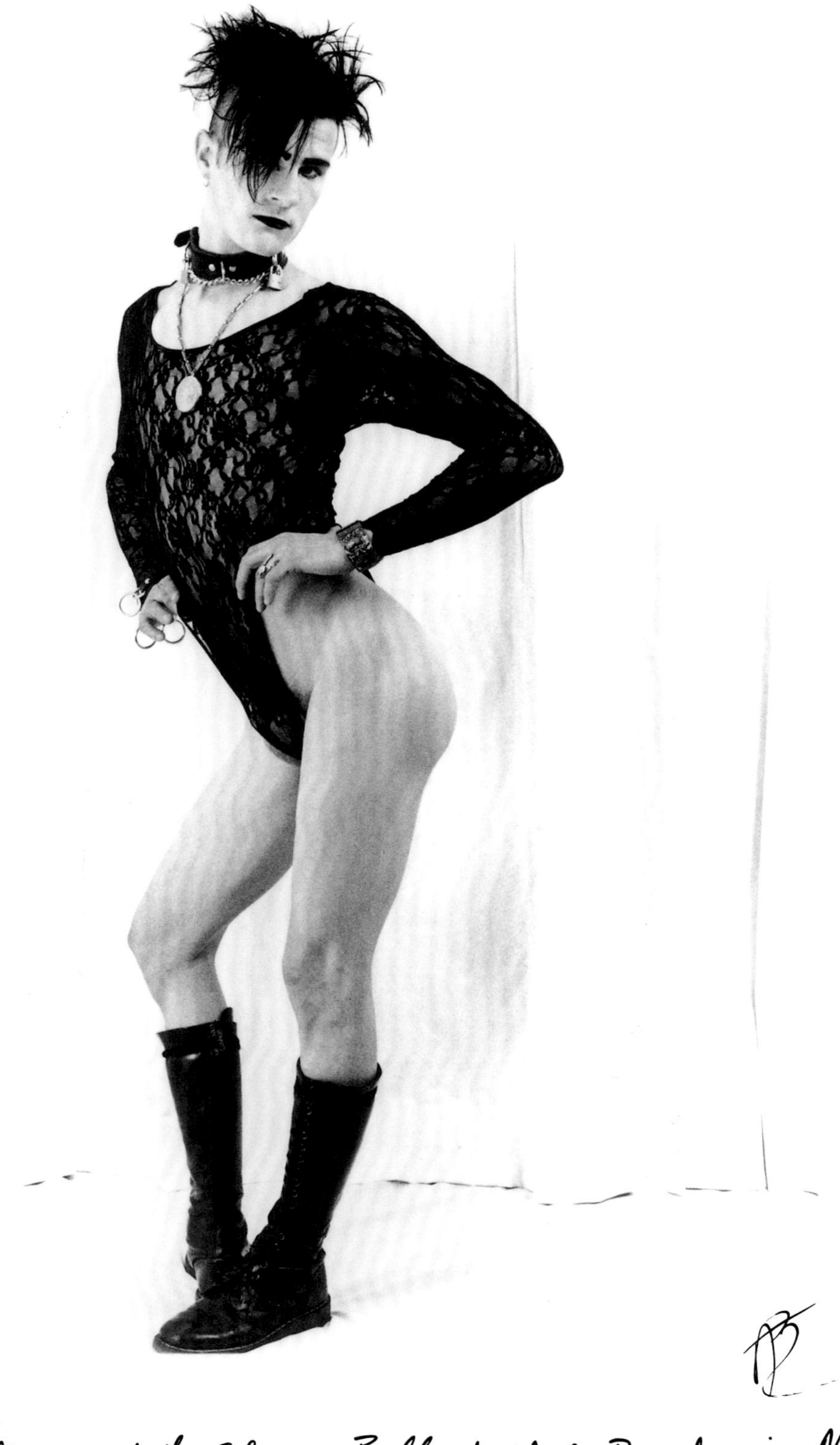

Ben '92

Ben materialized at the Sleeze Ball at Club Paradox in November of 1992. At this time he was supporting a son in Annapolis and had traveled a lot for his twenty years. This led to a description of a life in cellars, the economics of living on nothing—and drugs. An arresting tale involved the fate of a friend, a late night overdose, whose body was thrown in a dumpster to avoid police detection.

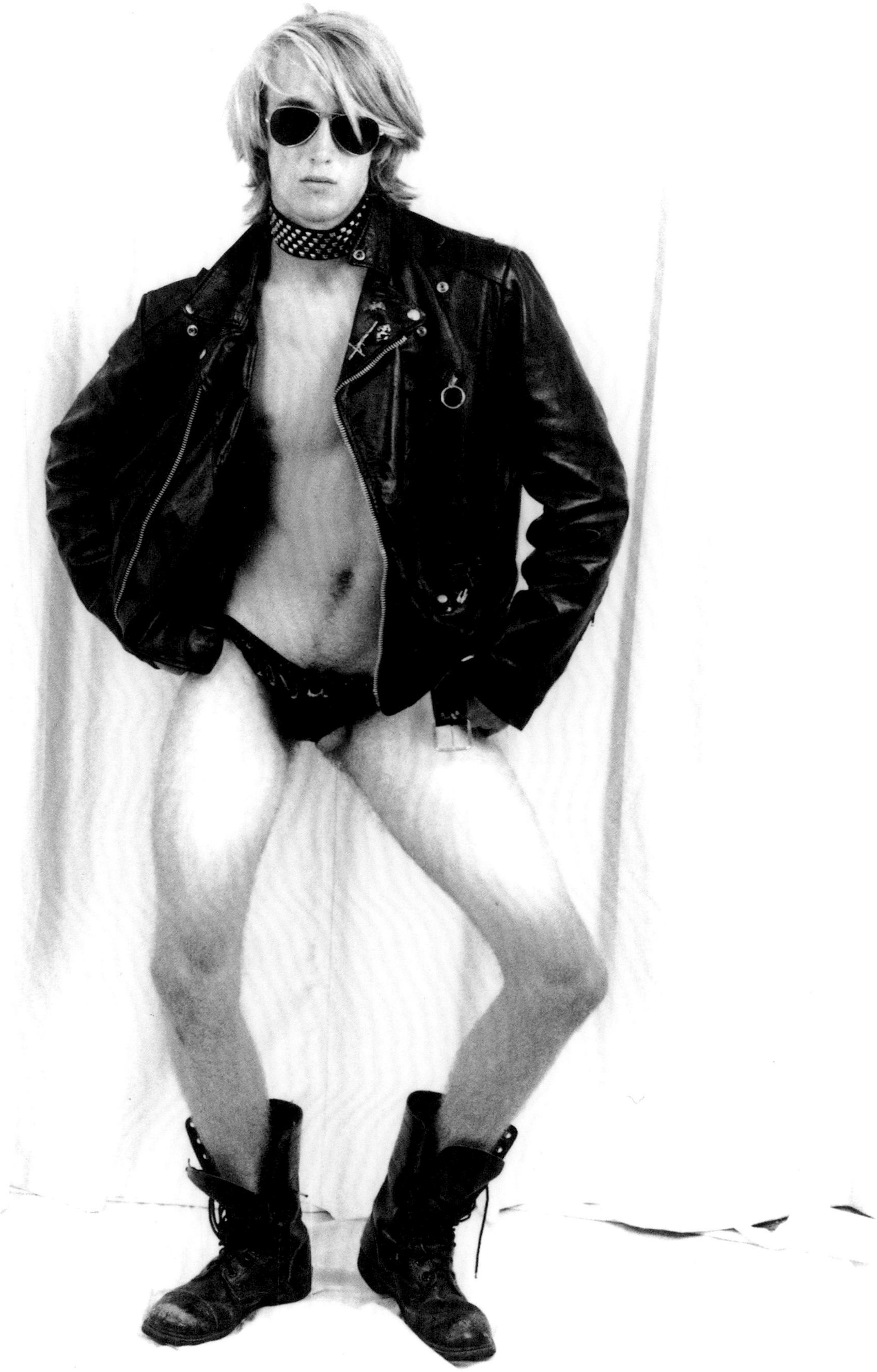

Matt

The boy across the street:
St. Paul Street

'91

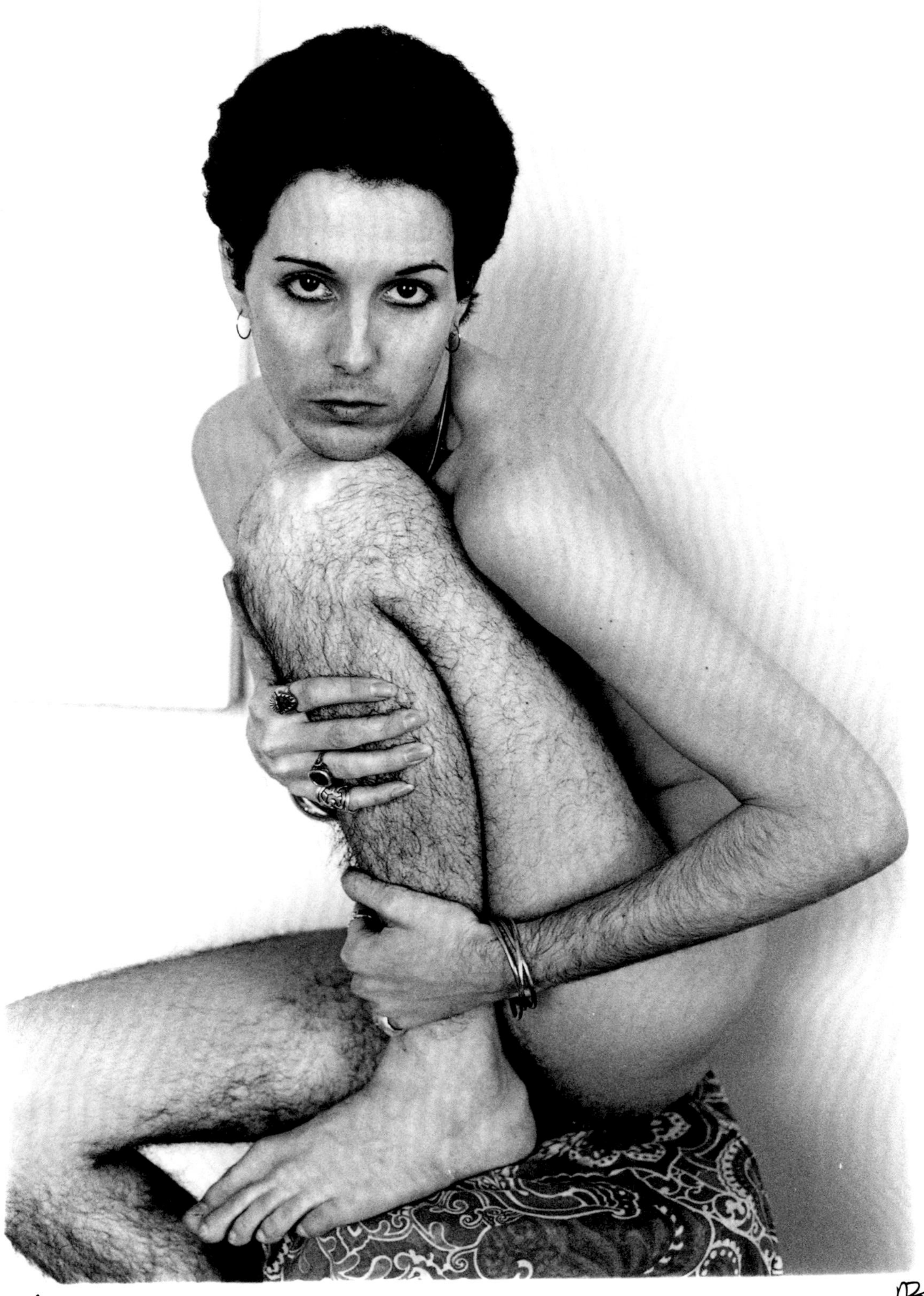

Laurence M. Doane

AB '76

Larry was an early subject for my camera. At this time he was living with Chuck in the second floor apartment of 23 E. Eager St. The bruise must be on the other arm. Closest friend: Roy Campbell. Gentle as spring violets.

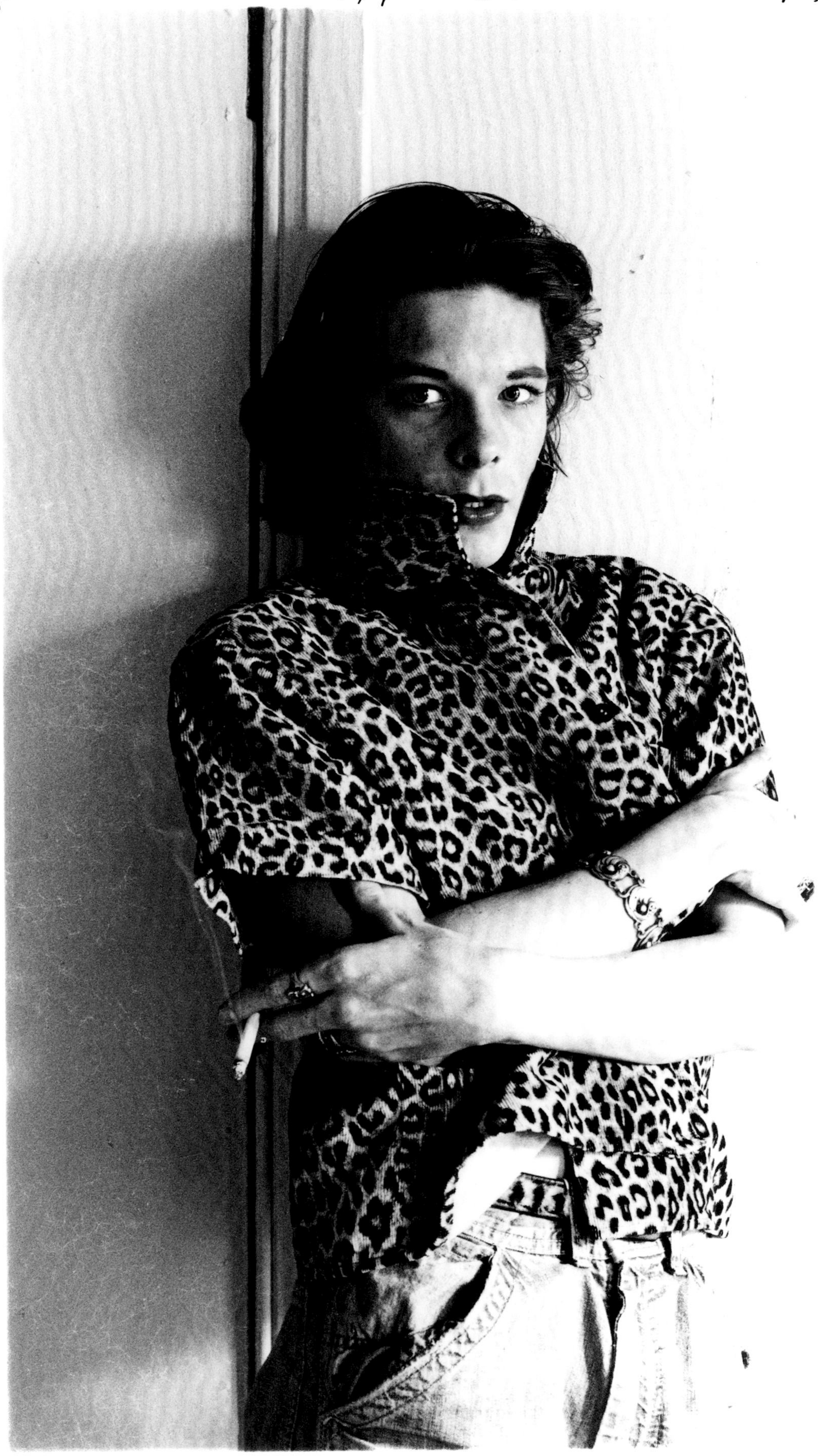

Todd had too many personalities, — and the lightest fingers in Charm City. He was abandoned by his mother at 10 yrs. old, given nothing, and became the abused, molested + very lonely product of a children's home. His was an outrageous fantasy world; manipulative, cold, inventive. He was on the streets of Baltimore (Park + Monument), pocketbook + make-up, hustling for drugs, cash + sex by 14. Here he is in 1975, at 21, as the young Katherine Hepburn and an early genius of thrift store chic. Todd's life became increasingly violent through drug + alcohol use and he died of AIDS in 1986 (or thereabouts), and not too many people, including Todd, gave a shit.

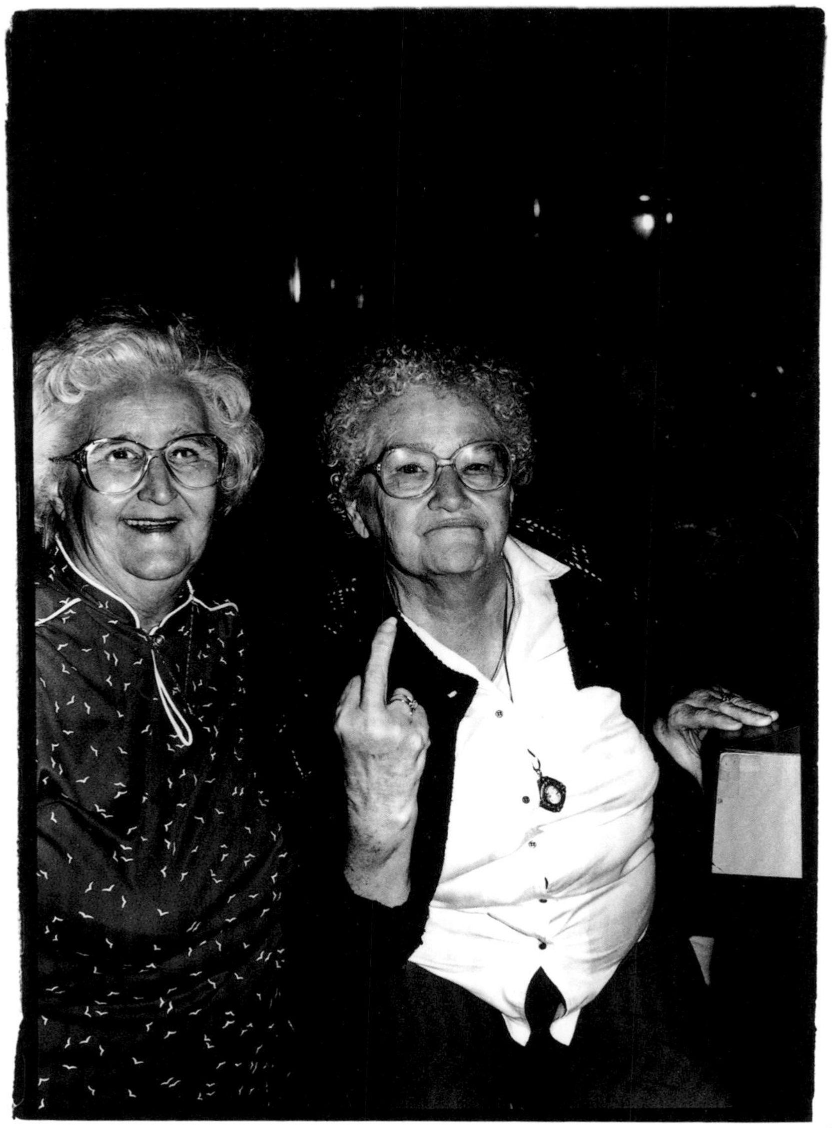

Rumors on Lombard St.

AZ '94

Benjamin Rush, a signer of the Declaration of Independence and therefore a founding father, wrote that masturbation caused poor eyesight, epilepsy, memory loss, tuberculosis, acne, bashfulness, nail biting, use of tobacco, bed wetting, idiocy, an appetite for meat, premature old age, a blighted body, impotence, premature ejaculation, dislike for intercourse and a ruined soul.

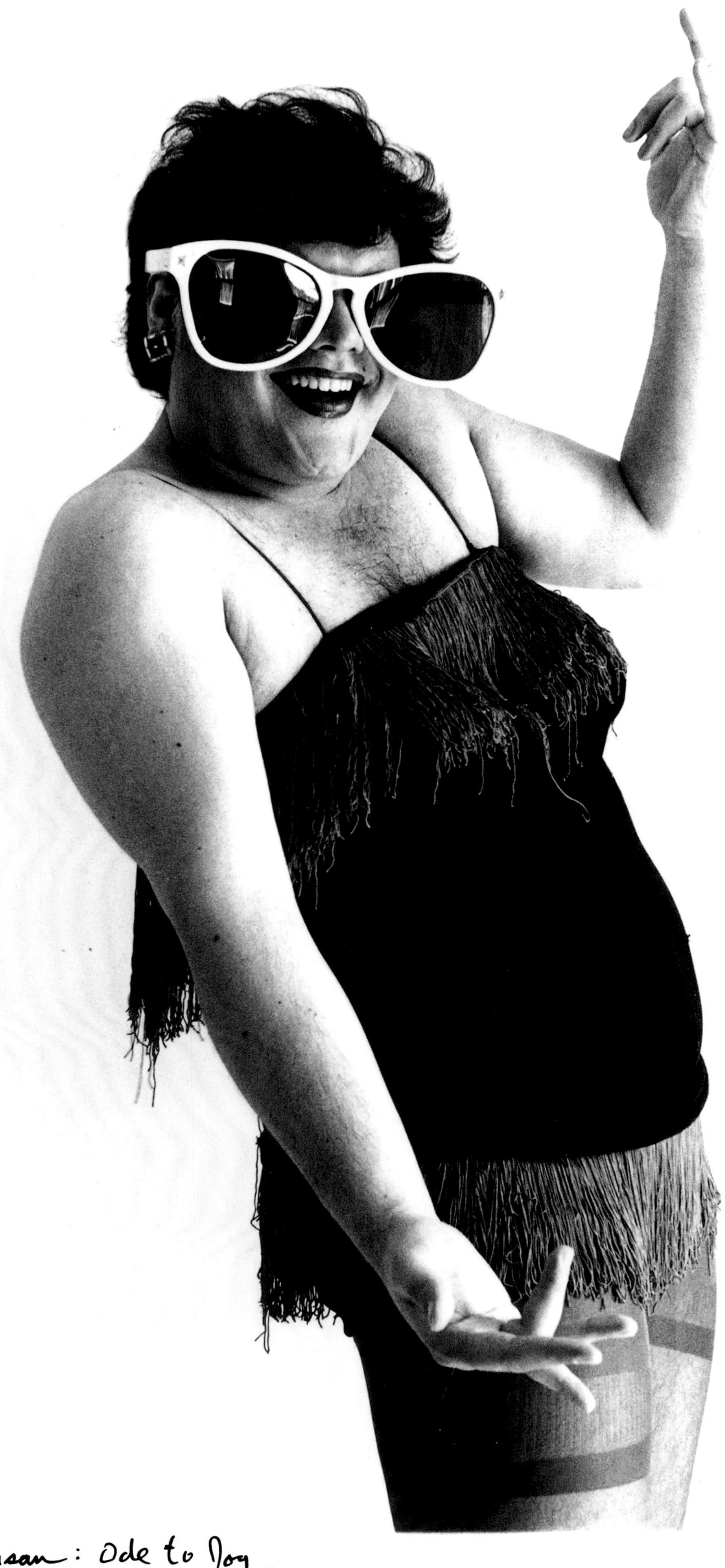

Mark Manalansan: Ode to Joy

Mark as he appeared in the Miss Hippo contest of 1980.

RC '80

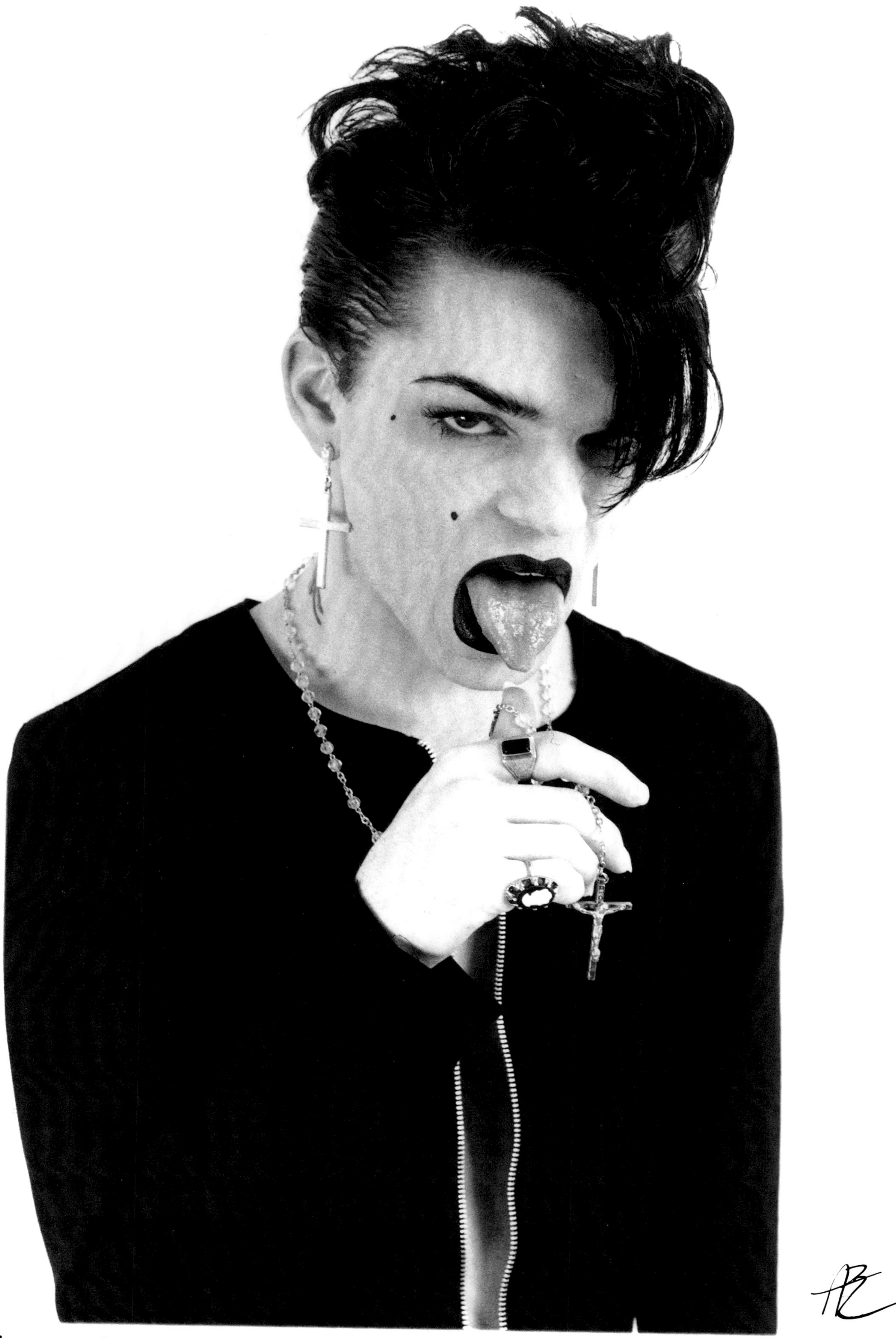

his holiness the paws – Finnegans Wake p-91
Johnathan '91

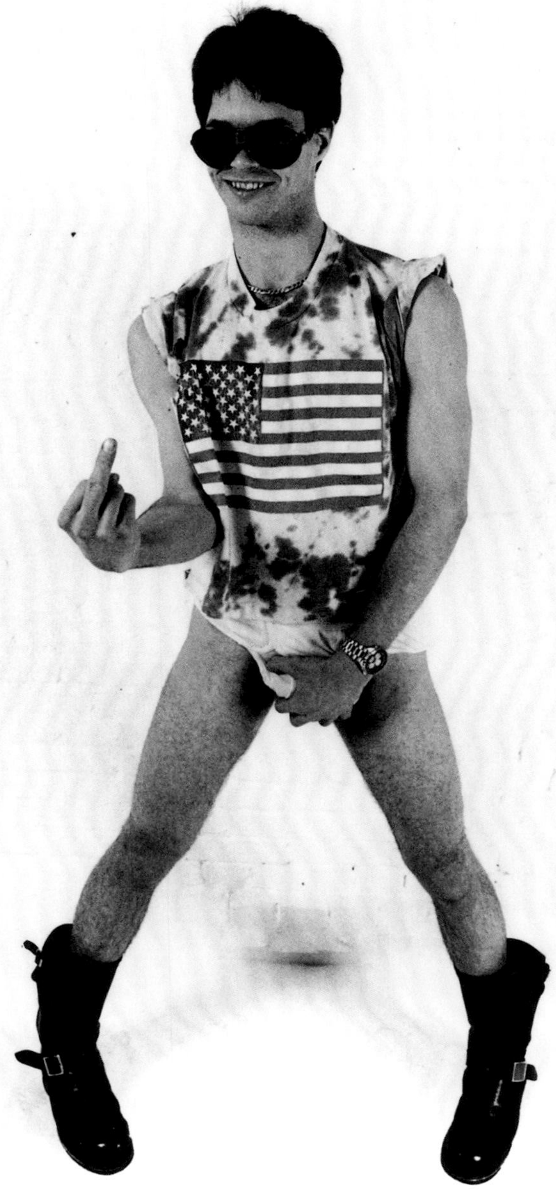

Billie: Captain America

AR '94

Born: Feb. 1971. Since the age of fifteen when his parents split up and his girlfriend died, Billy had a way with women, alcohol, drugs and cars (fire chicken). Mostly joyriding. Mustangs and Tempos. And firing cocaine. Without the aid of the born again set or the head doctors, he got his life together at 20, reversed his habits and got a job.

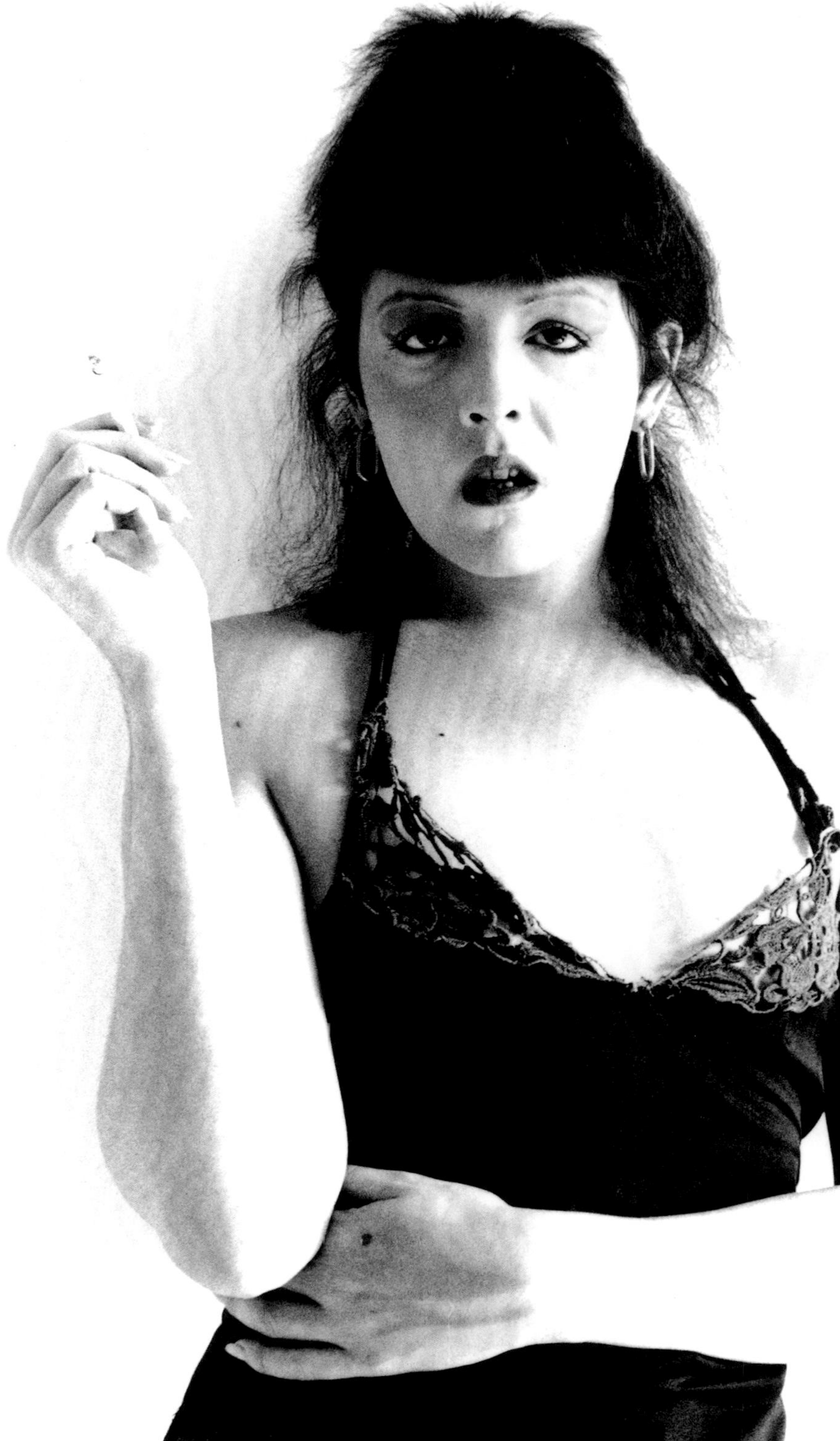

Leonard '79
Miss Lena

a large, visible working girl on the scene big time throughout the seventies — in the clubs & on the streets. Particularly, Charles & Eager Sts.; close by the Hippo. He retired Miss Lena in the 80's and as of 1994 works in a diner — as a man.

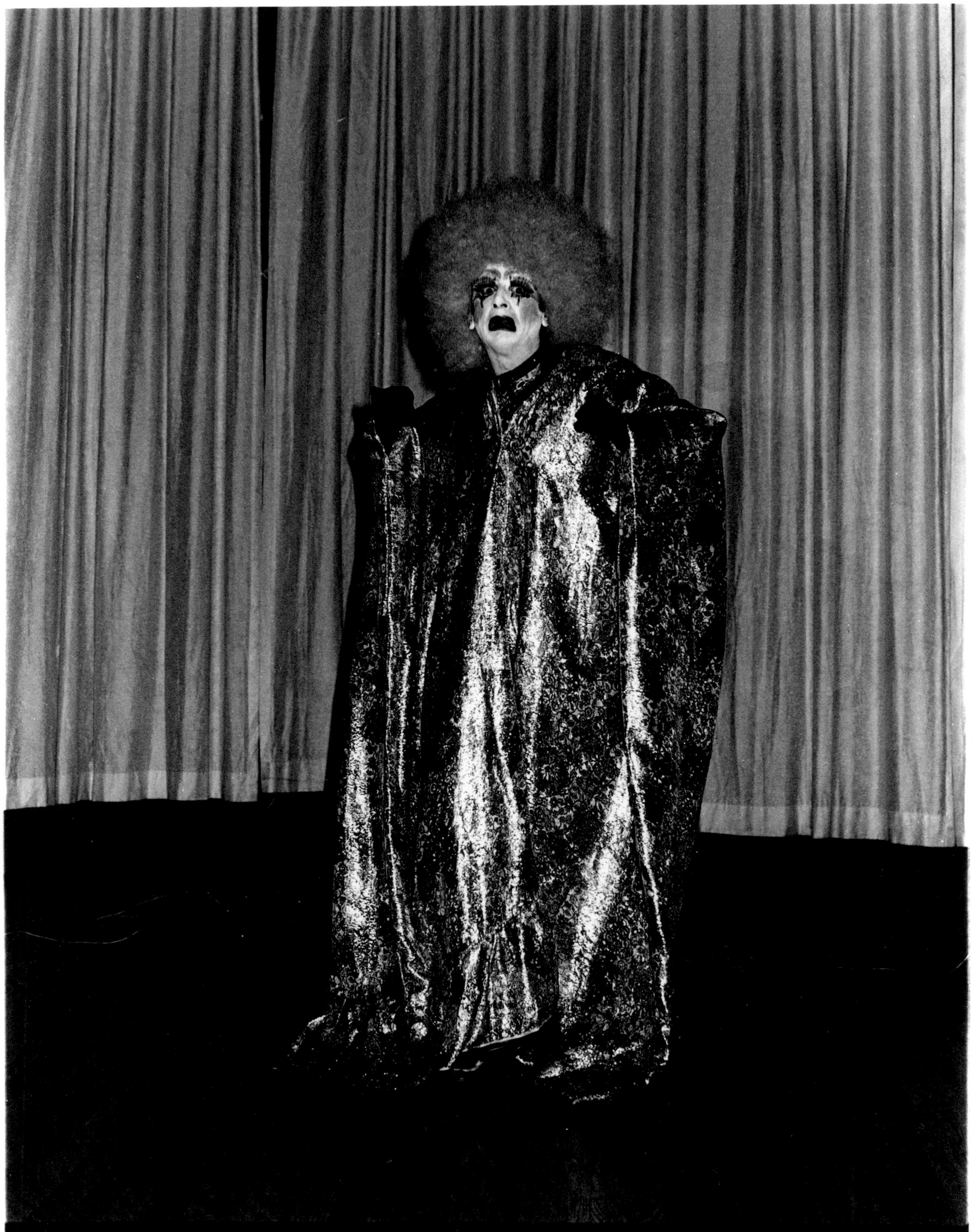

Alan Lozito - of Saratoga: Washington D.C.: 1975
The talented founder of the three-man comedy group, Saratoga. They played the Hippo and a number of D.C. + New York bars around the time of this photograph. Alan died in N.Y.C. of AIDS in the late 80's.

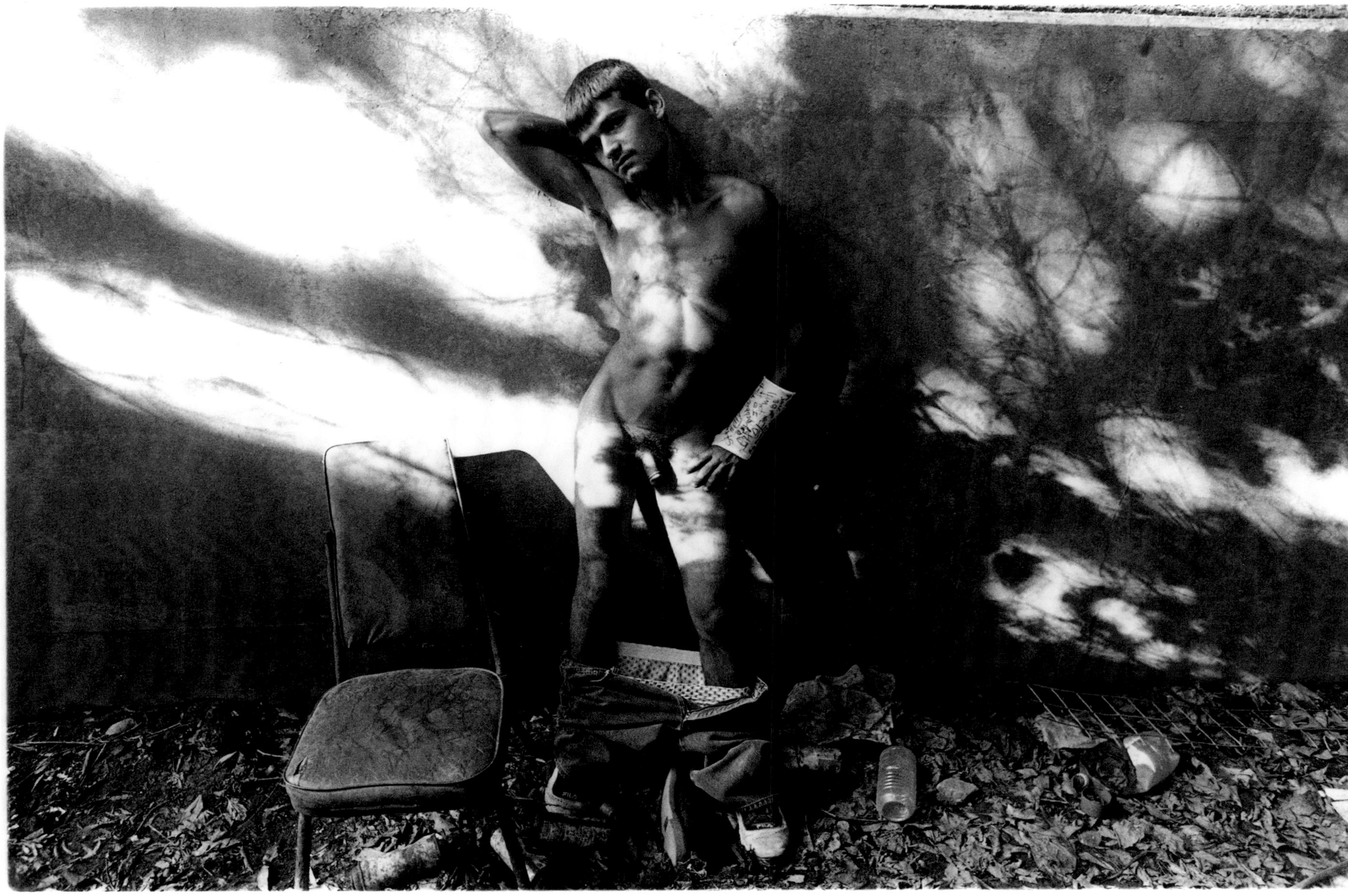

Big Daddy: Sunday: Under an Interstate

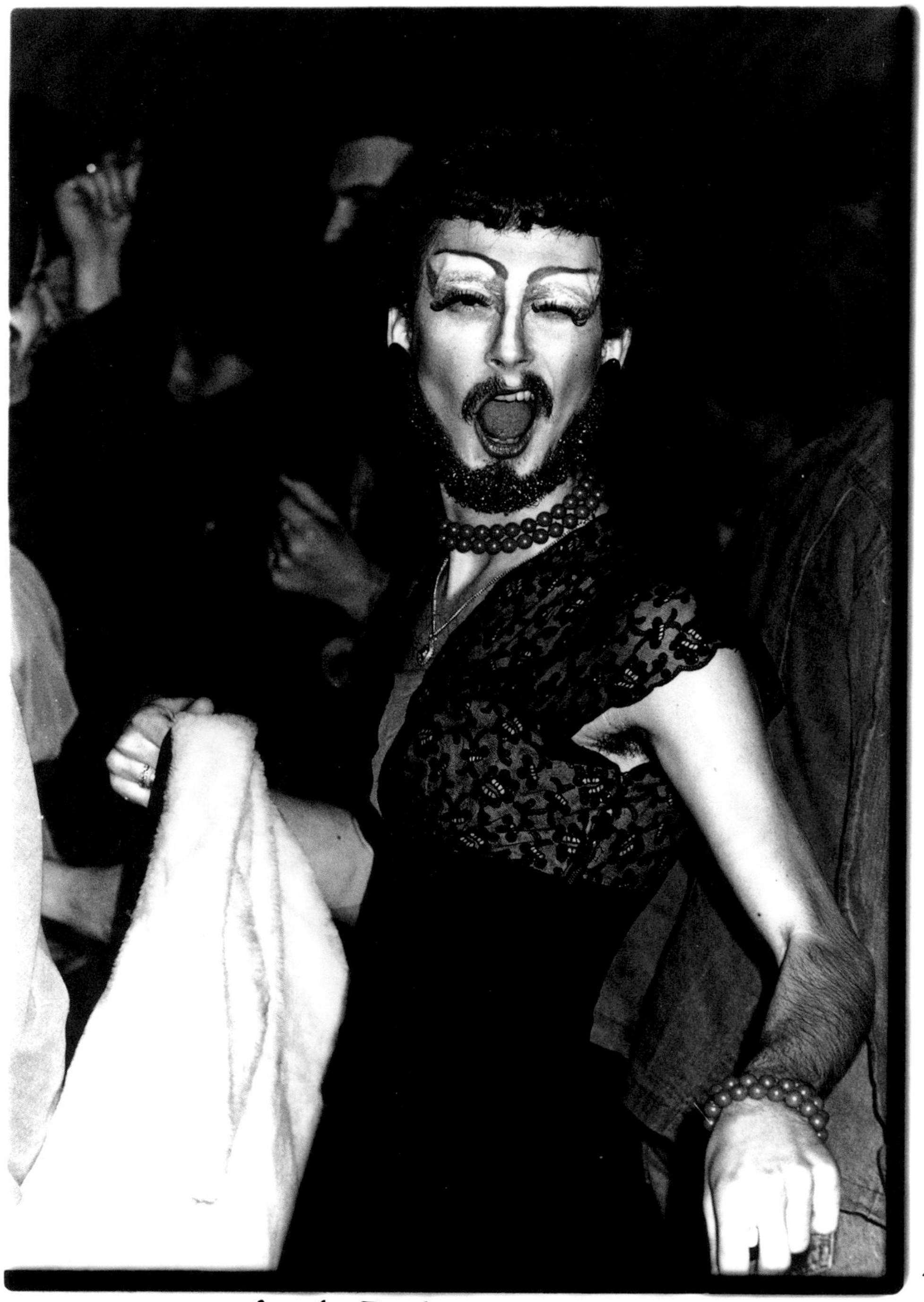

the Denim + Pearls Ball – Dec. 75, at the Alcazar

Jesus wept: and no wonder, by Christ.

Ulysses – p. 38

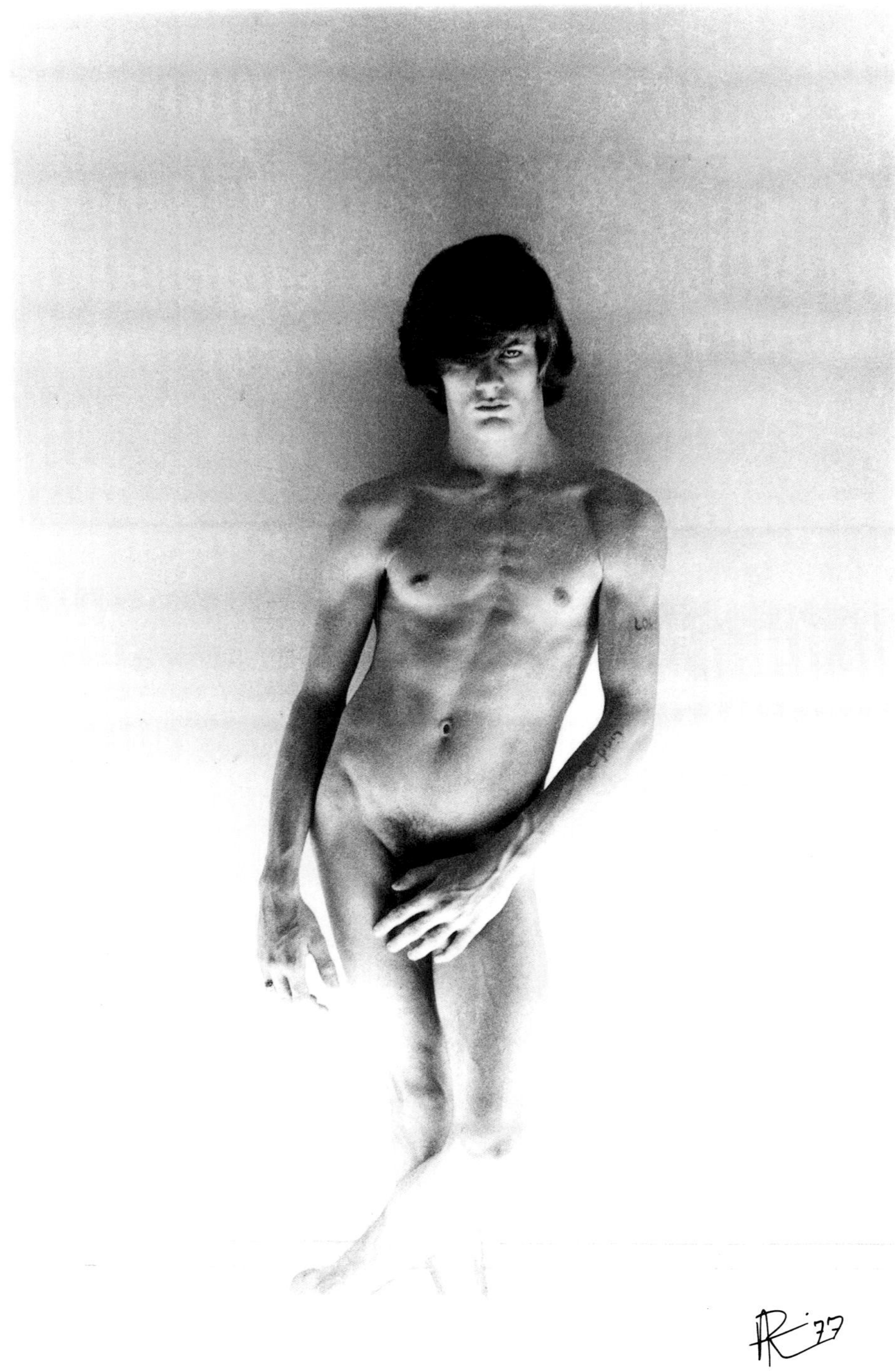

Amos,

Just a few lines to say Hello! I was very Happy but shocked to see your letter! How are you doing? I reliz its been along Time, but I have a good memory! I'm glad to here that my photograph's came out good. why don't you send me a few? I'm sending you a small picture of me, its not the best one but its all I have, cause these pictures cost $2.00 each and I havent any money nor any one to rely on! I will explain my reason for being in Jail for the next few lines. When I left Baltimore I ran into this chick and she fucked over me in more ways than one So I worked for her father's company which is Globe Security. So I was on Hairon and Robbed her father of $38,000.00. I was arrested 3-weeks later and returned $37,000.00 Back to her father and I bought myself a 1971 Barracuda plymouth. when I saw the Judge he sentenced me to 1½ to 3 years at the State Correctional Institution Camp Hill, pa. When I was here for 1½ and went up for Parole the Board fucked over me and gave me 15-months more to do. So I was very hurt and upset, and tryed to kill a parole agent. So I was charged with atemped to kill a state offical the Judge sentenced me to 10 months to 2 years running consecutive meaning after my 1½ to 3 years! I feel Bad because I never intended to hurt the girl just let her know that I was hurting! I miss being high and drinking and being able to drive my car and live freely! can you understand that I'm not a criminal I did'nt relize my wrong doing til I was arrested! I hope that you - Brad & Kay can forgive me and give me another chance with you all? I don't write to any body but you all now because I was thinking of the good times we all had together... and I'm hoping that will have more to come? Please forgive me, it will never happen again! I'm not doing so well and can't because I need things and can't get them with my looks! I can't accept any package's at all. if I need things I charge to my prison account and whenever I recieve money the deduct it from that So far I'm in $85.75¢ dept and don't care, because I don't have it and can't get it from any one! I recieved $2.00 so far since I'r been here and couldn't have it because it was cash and not a Money Order for me! Sounds crazy right? But cash could buy all the dope in the Jail! I'm scared because if Someone doesn't help me pay my debt then they'll get other inmates to hurt me. like Breaking my legs or arms I'm twenty two years old and never had a Broken Bone in my Body.. Do me one small favor and help me - But never tell anyone about the Jail Because I could get into alot of serious trouble and I'll never Make parole So please hush-hush. Just help me! okay? I can't get anyone to help me cause I have No-one! I asked you to send me Some of them pictures. its cool to do So I have a guard Who'll be waiting on them and he'll do any thing I ask him to do. So please send me a few nude or not nude okay? 1-nude if your sending me any! the rest must be presentible okay? I'm on the Jail's Boxing team and my record is 13 wins 3-loses. 8 knockouts and 1-Dessission I do this to keep in shape and to keep myself alive! Please help me out. Write me soon! I want to remain as yours amos - But your have to decide and help me - If you help me then I'll repay you in Bed once I'm out of Jail my word!

Love Always

John H

4-16-79

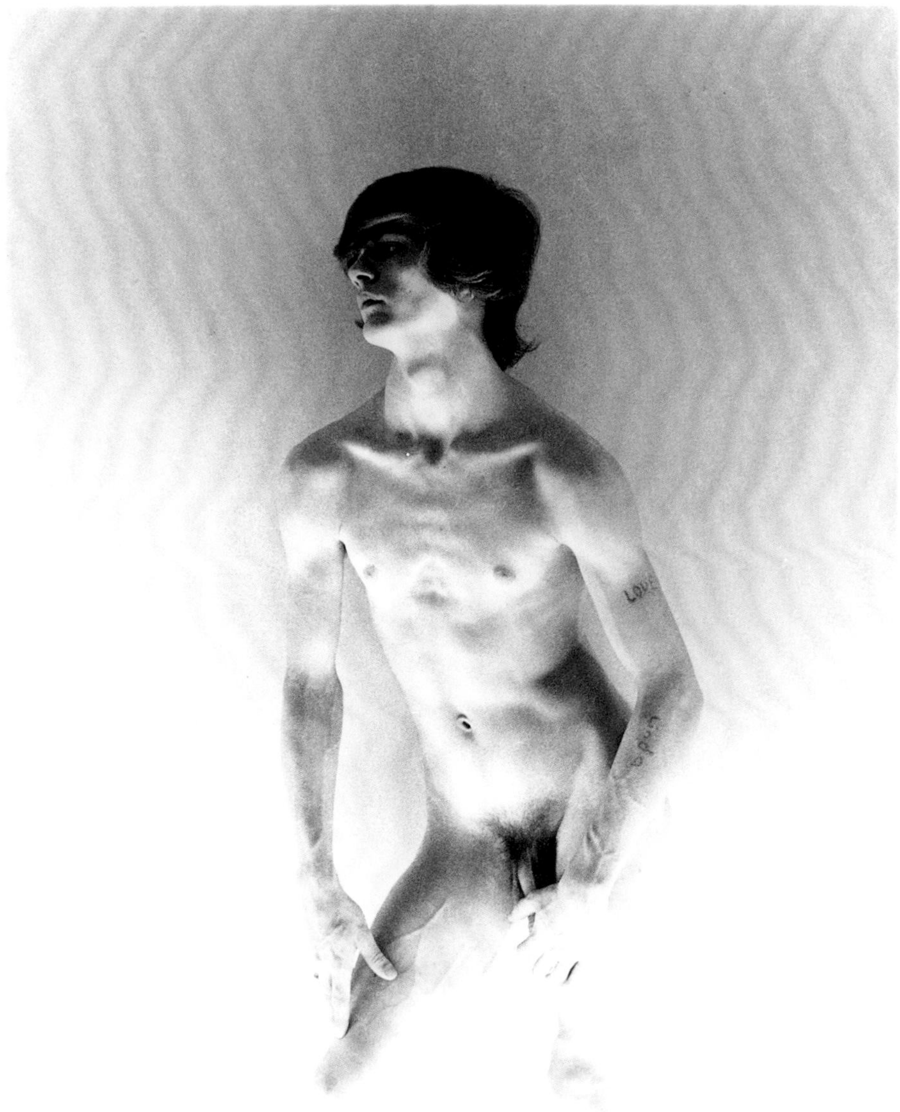

John

AB '77

Amos,

5-5-79

Just a few lines to say Hello again! How are you doing? Sure hope your doing fine! as for my self I'm more confussed than any thing. I mean you wrote to me, asking me to explain why I'm in Jail, and When I do, you never responded back, Why? are you against me or with me? I was very Serious when I said I'd like for it to be me and you. I'll do any thing you say even stay with you when I get out. Amos you can't close me out of your life. I'm not a criminal I'm a person with feelings or can't you see that? I really need for you to help me and we will belong to <u>each</u> <u>other</u> forever. I'm not saying these things from the top of my head I'm speaking from the heart and fellings! Are you gonna help me or leave me hanging? I still want Some of those pictures, that you took of me, is that okay with you? I need you and want you so please write to me and lets discuss this over to a agreable level. I'm still in dept of $85.75¢ if you can't give all give what you can!

Sincerly yours
Love
John
CH

over
↓↓↓

I wont write any more letters to you unless I recieve one from you. John CH

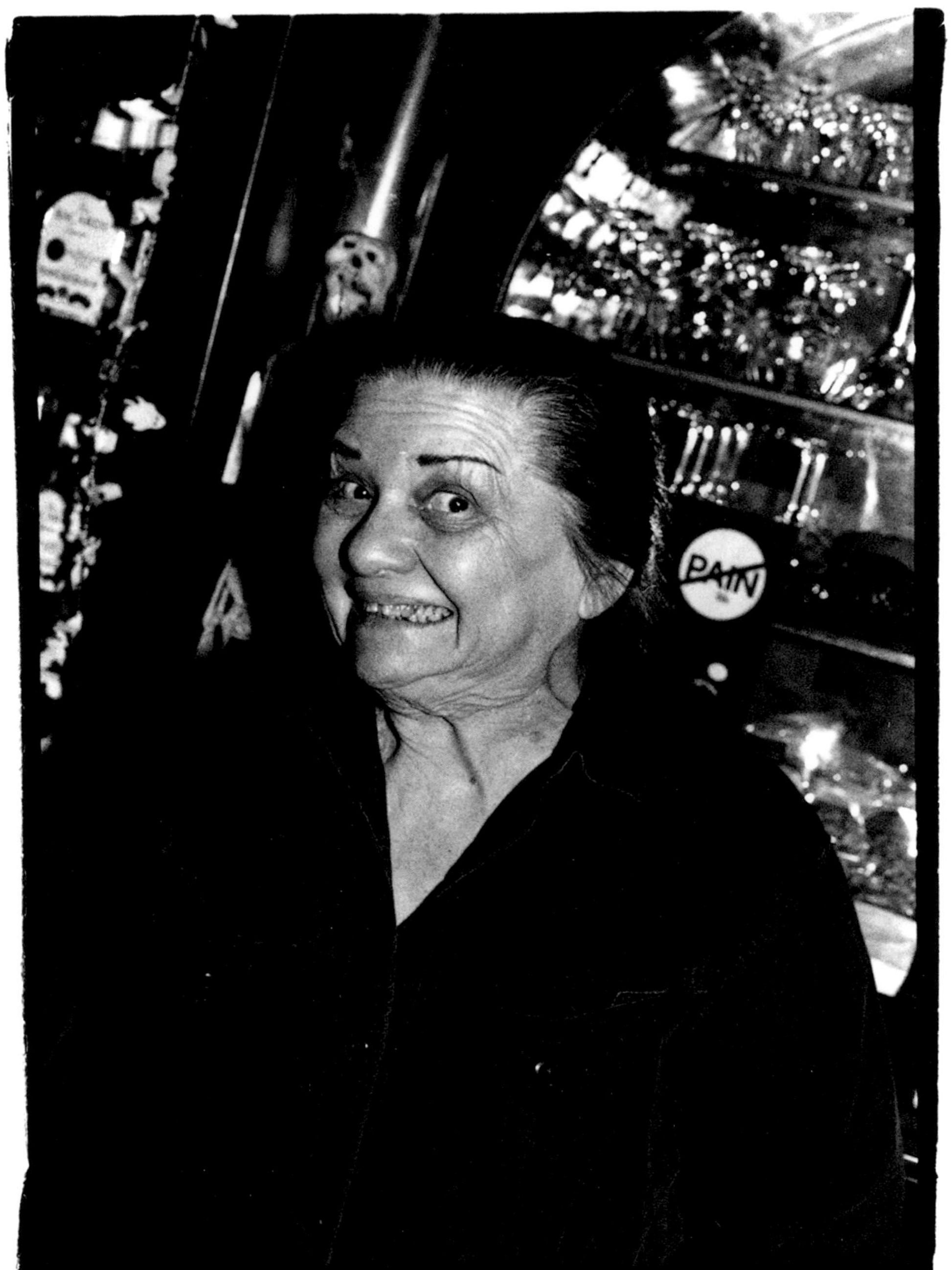

Esther Martin

AR '90

The most politically incorrect bar owner within shooting distance of North Ave. – and the bold architect of the cunt-hair martini. Esther worked at the old Club Charles at the corner of Charles + Preston STs. in the early 40's and then at the 21 Club (across the street from the Lord Baltimore Hotel) in 1950–51. She then bought the present Club Charles in 1951 when it was called Charles Seafood and then became the Wigwam. Anyone who is anyone in either direction has been here – improved their vocabulary or run up a bar tab.

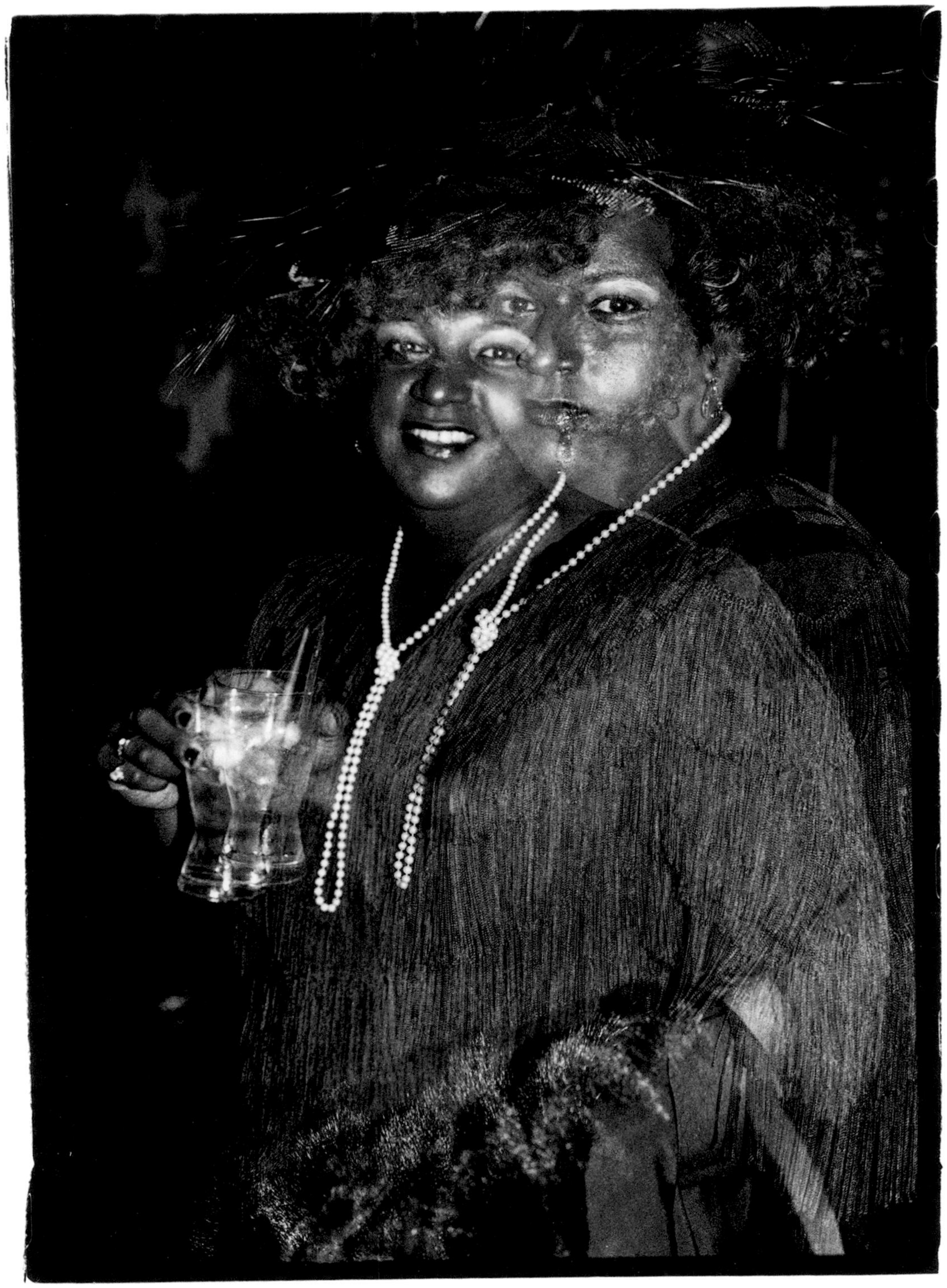

At Club Atlantis

AR '89

church lady, after too much knotty head.

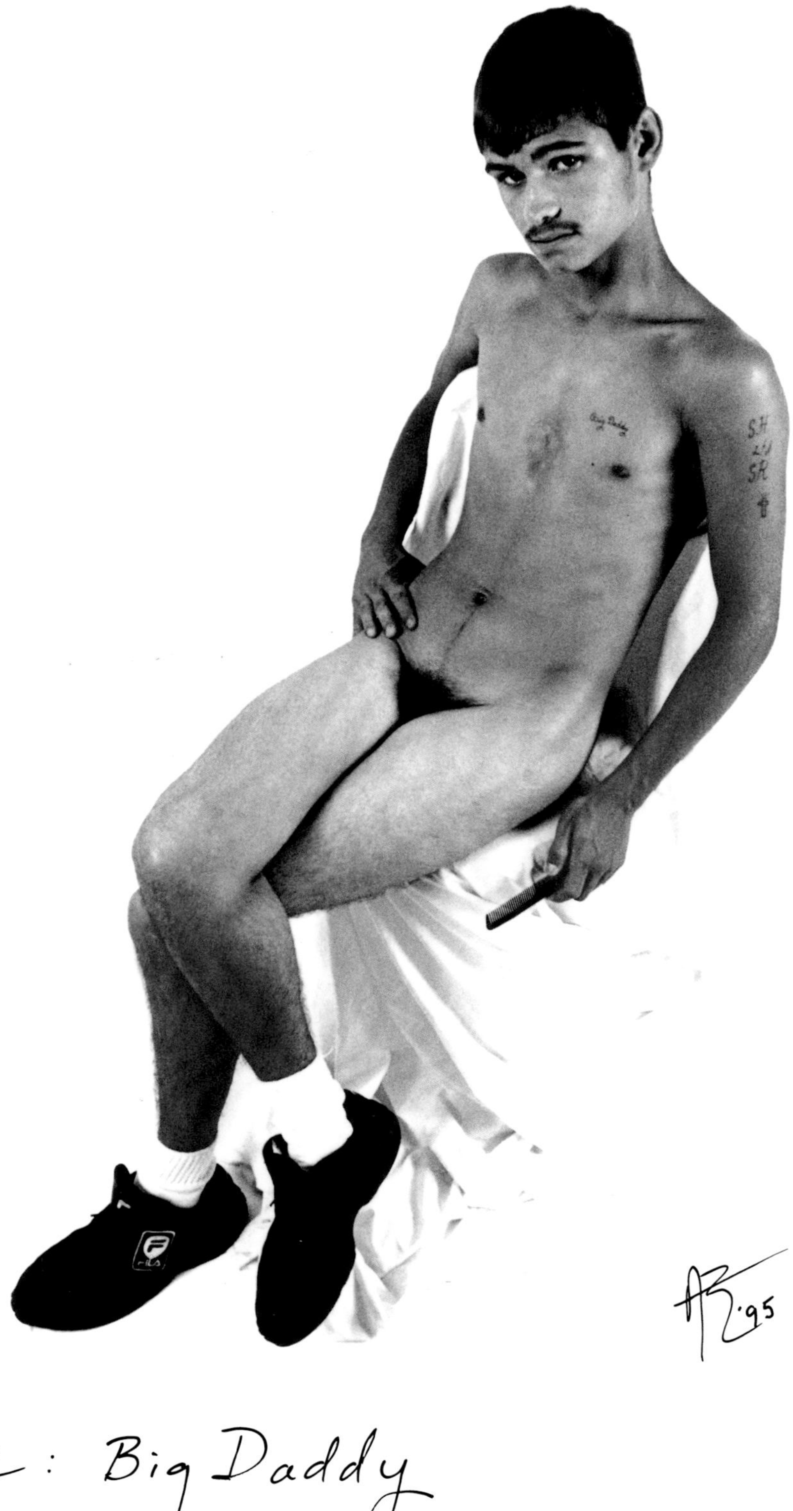

Steve : Big Daddy

Boy with a comb : effectively street-wise
with a short fuse.

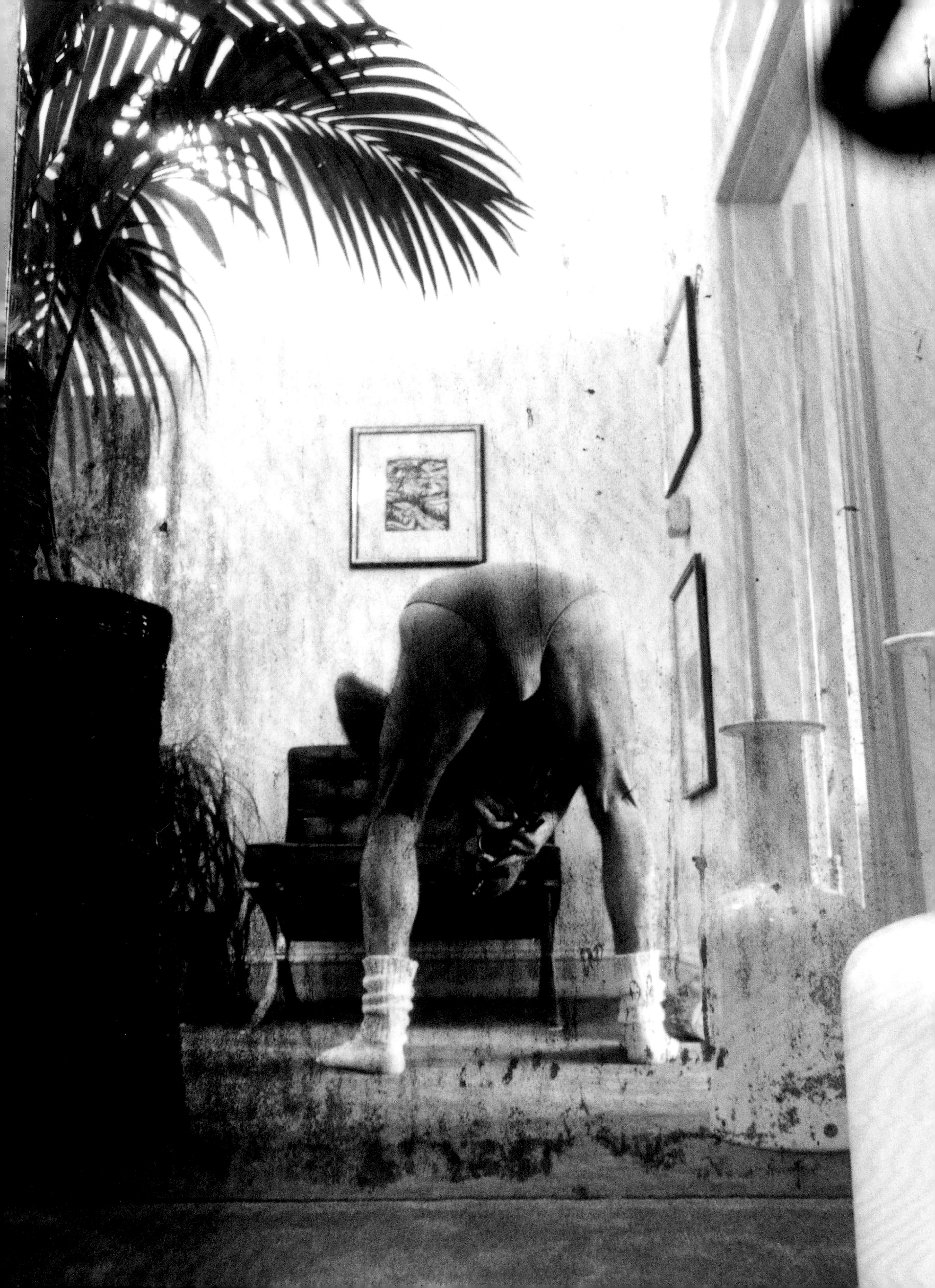

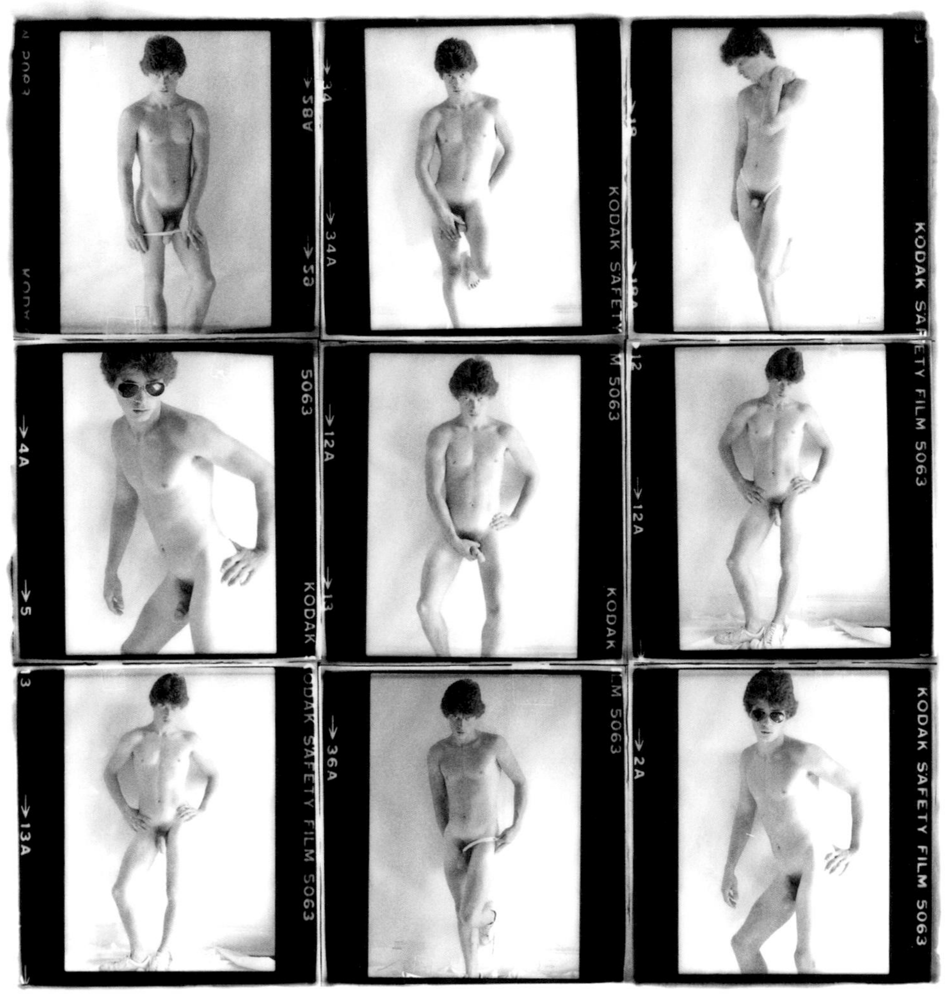

Birds
of
Paradise

1982
1994

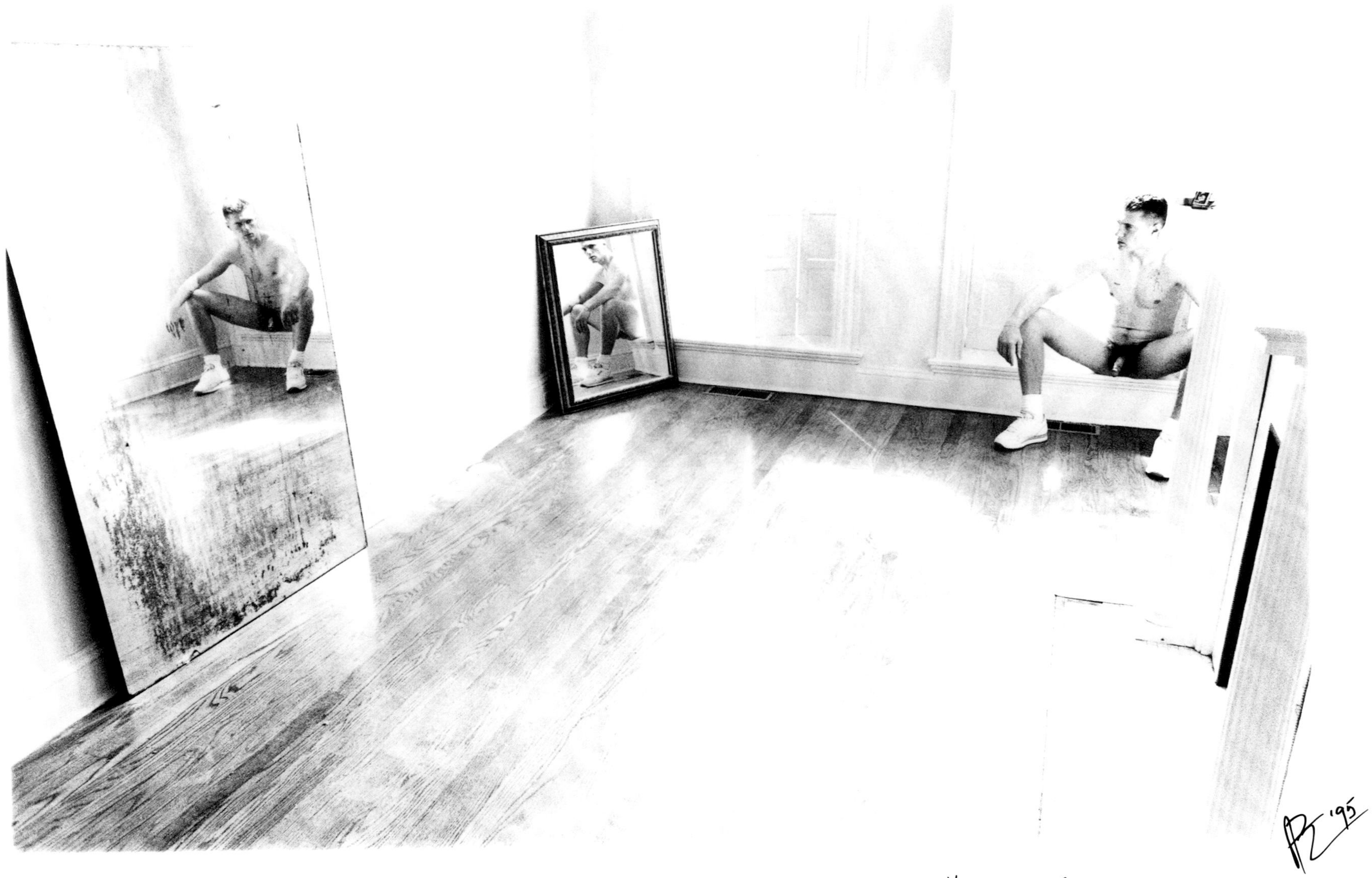

Sonny was born in 1974, the same year his parents split up. His father taught him boxing to survive on Baltimore's grim westside until a street brawl left him in a coma for 7 years. He died in 1994. Sonny hustled men, used heroin, occasionally beating and robbing "fruits". Home is with mother – an abusive relationship. He can neither read nor write – nor work.

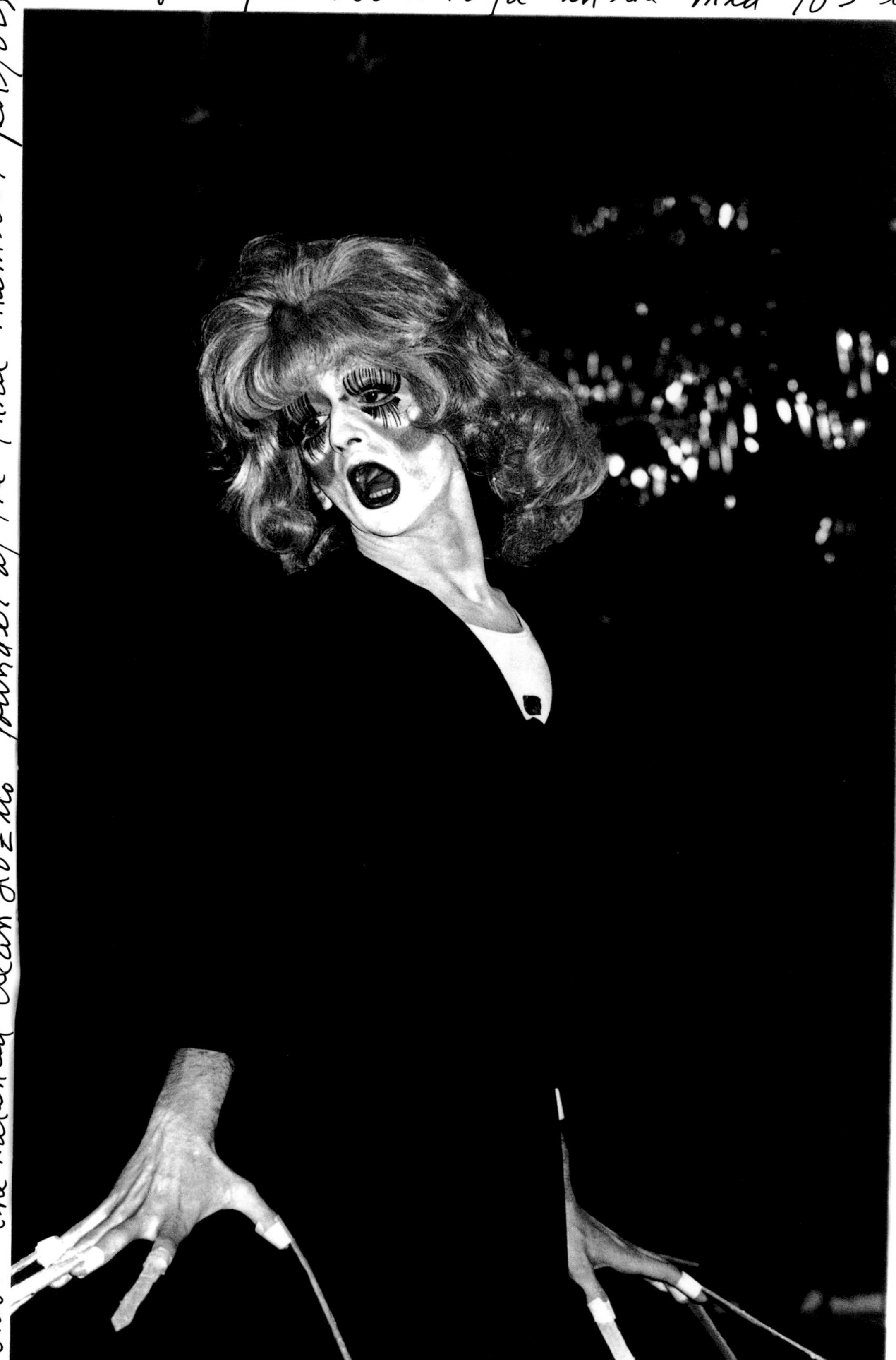

This is the talented Alan Lozito founder of the three-member performance group "Saratoga" in the mid 70's which played the gay clubs of D.C., NYC, NJ + Baltimore. Home base was his mother's apartment at the corner of the eponymous Jane + Hudson Sts., NY. Alan's hypnotic stage presence masked a lonely, chaotic + self-destructive personality, unrelieved by comic projection + drugs. He died of AIDS in 1986 at the same apartment in which he was born.

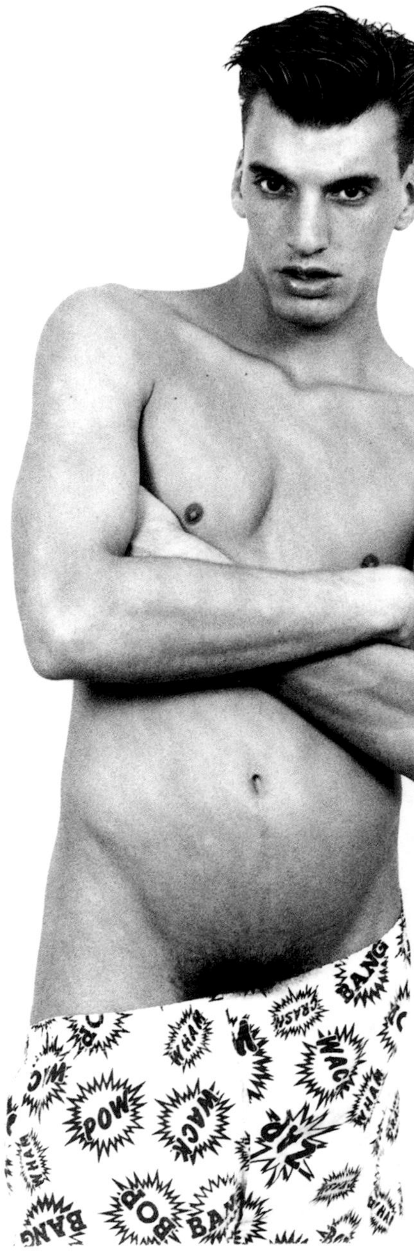

guy: porn star

AR '90

You could say that Guy's career as a male entertainer began on a Sunday in 1989 at Club Atlantis in Baltimore. His father had recently died and he was living with his mother. He had had a few drinks and was coaxed onto the performance bar by other dancers for the first time. Guy danced regularly in Baltimore for a while and then went to "La Cage" in D.C. He teamed up with a very expensive dancer, Scott, who helped with his bookings in N.Y.C., Florida and the west coast. "Goin' Down on the Farm" in 1991 is one of the videos of this period in L.A. There was a lot of money, a lot of drugs and a lot of entertaining & high-living. A lot of missed engagements — and time out in drug re-hab. Guy was a well-intentioned boy whose life daily reflected his mental disorganization. He lived out bizarre situations that most of us only read about.

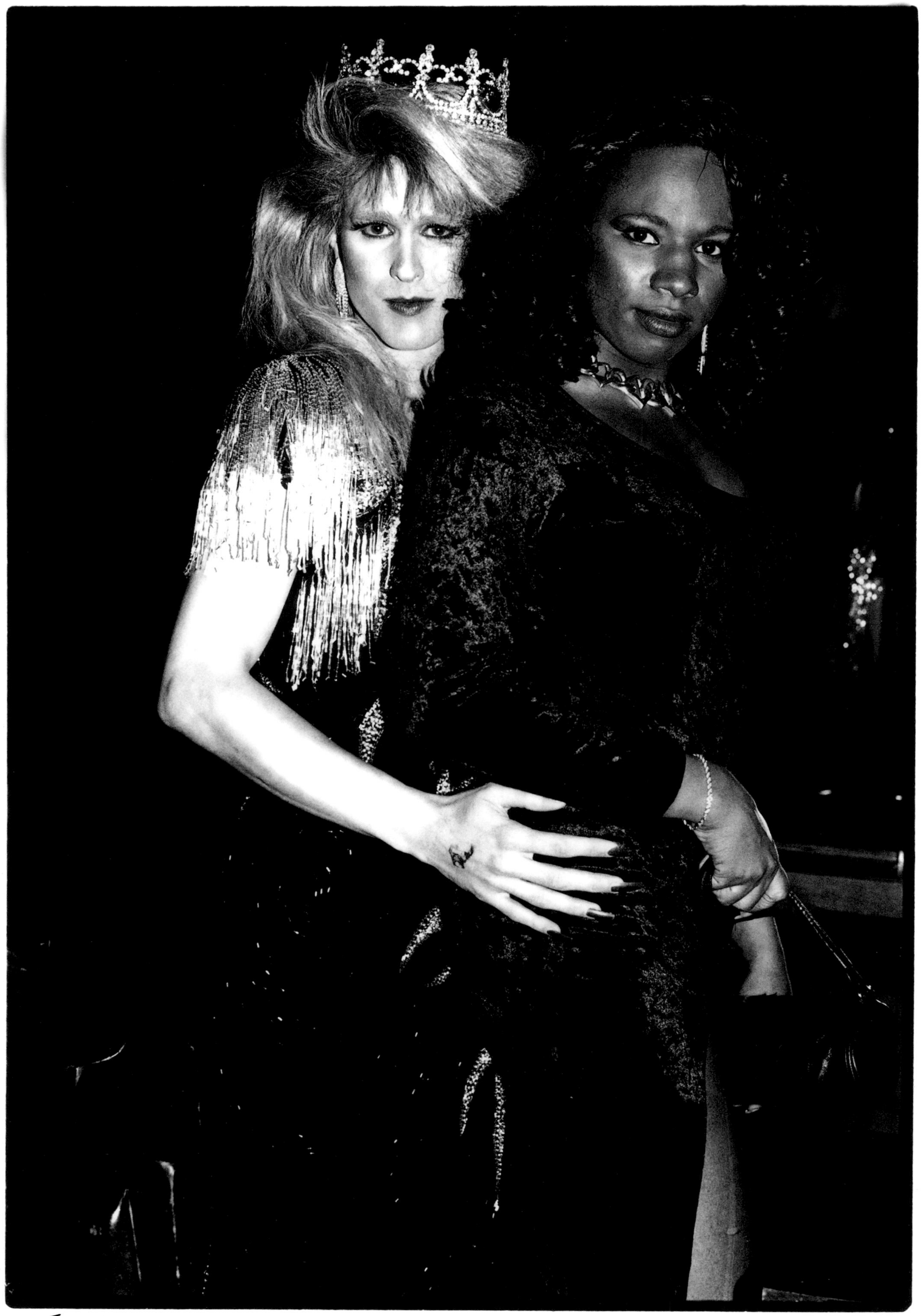

Two Ladies at the Hippo : Baltimore : October   AR '93

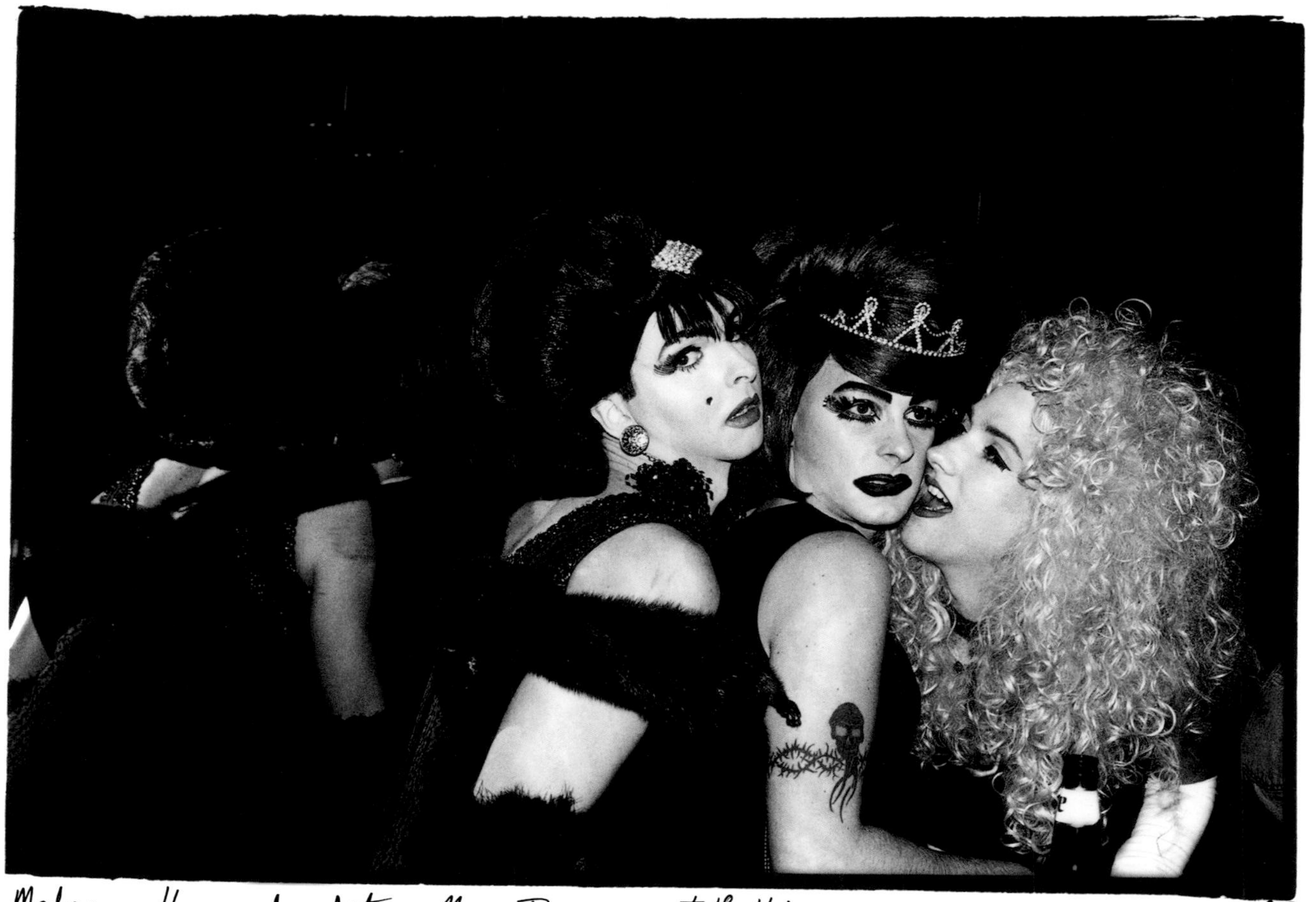

Medusa, Hermaphroditee, Miss Piss – at the Hippo

'93

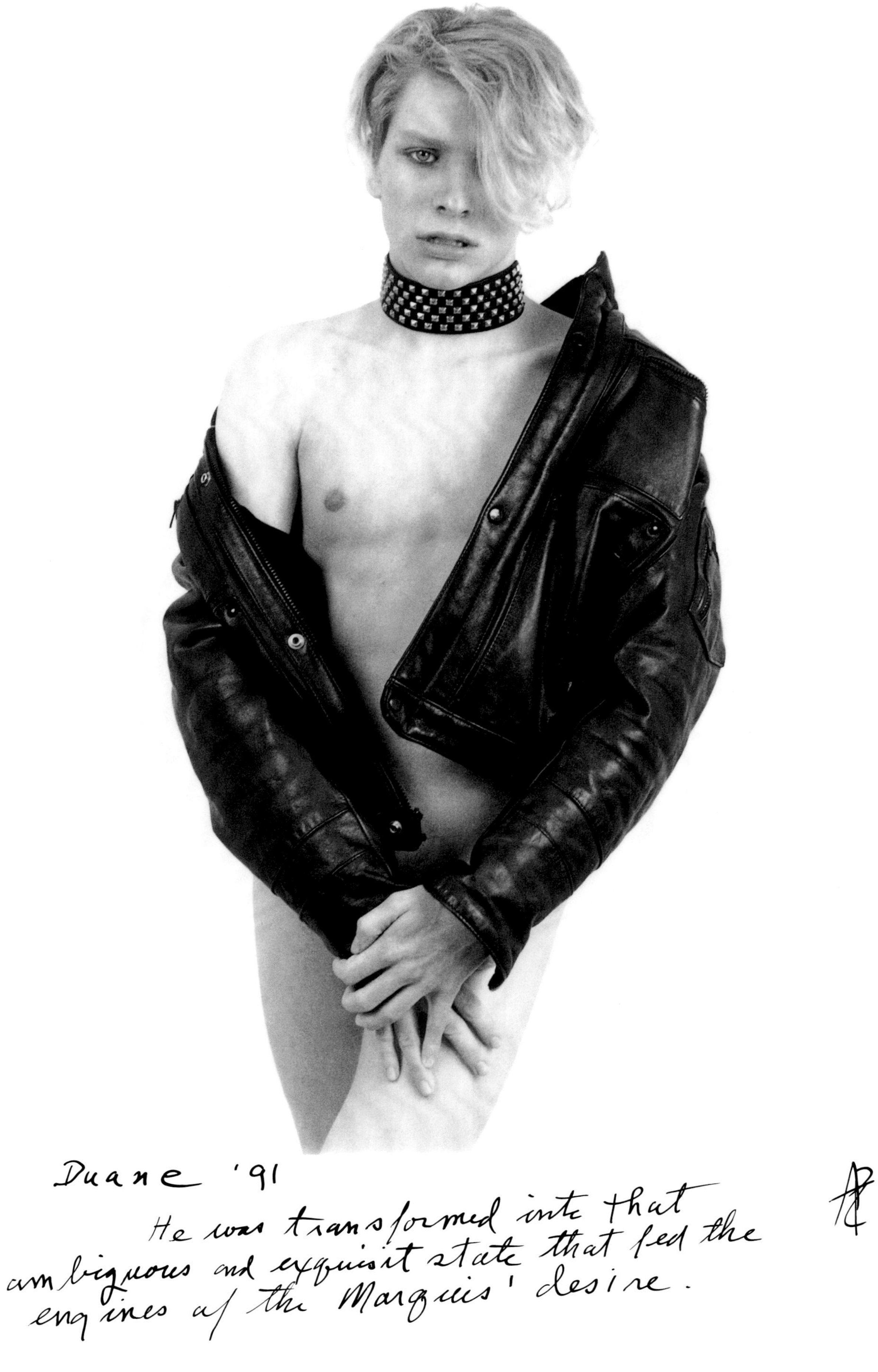
Duane '91
He was transformed into that ambiguous and exquisit state that fed the engines of the Marquis' desire.

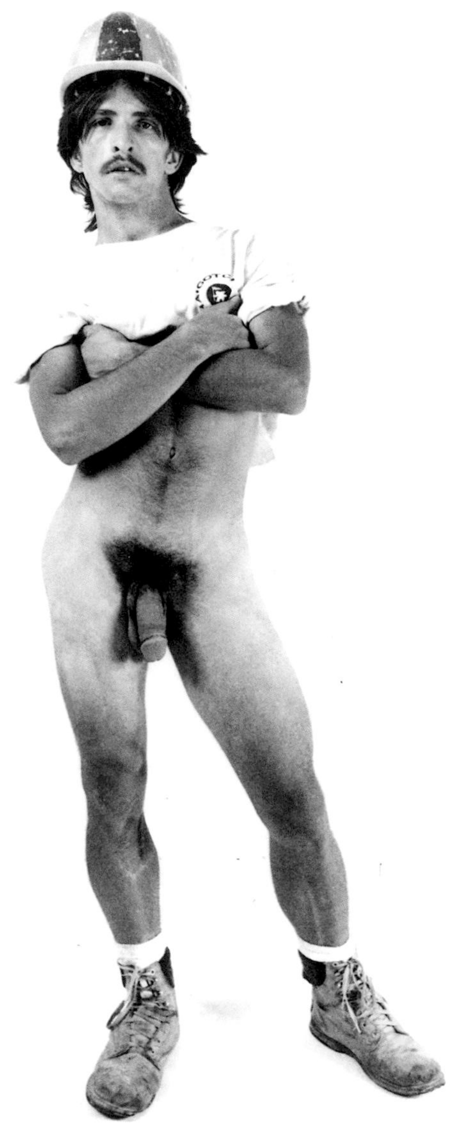

AR '93

Tony

Death Angel

Attractive in a damaged way! This is what every gentel blue-collar mother warns her teenage son (or daughter) about. Rough trade!

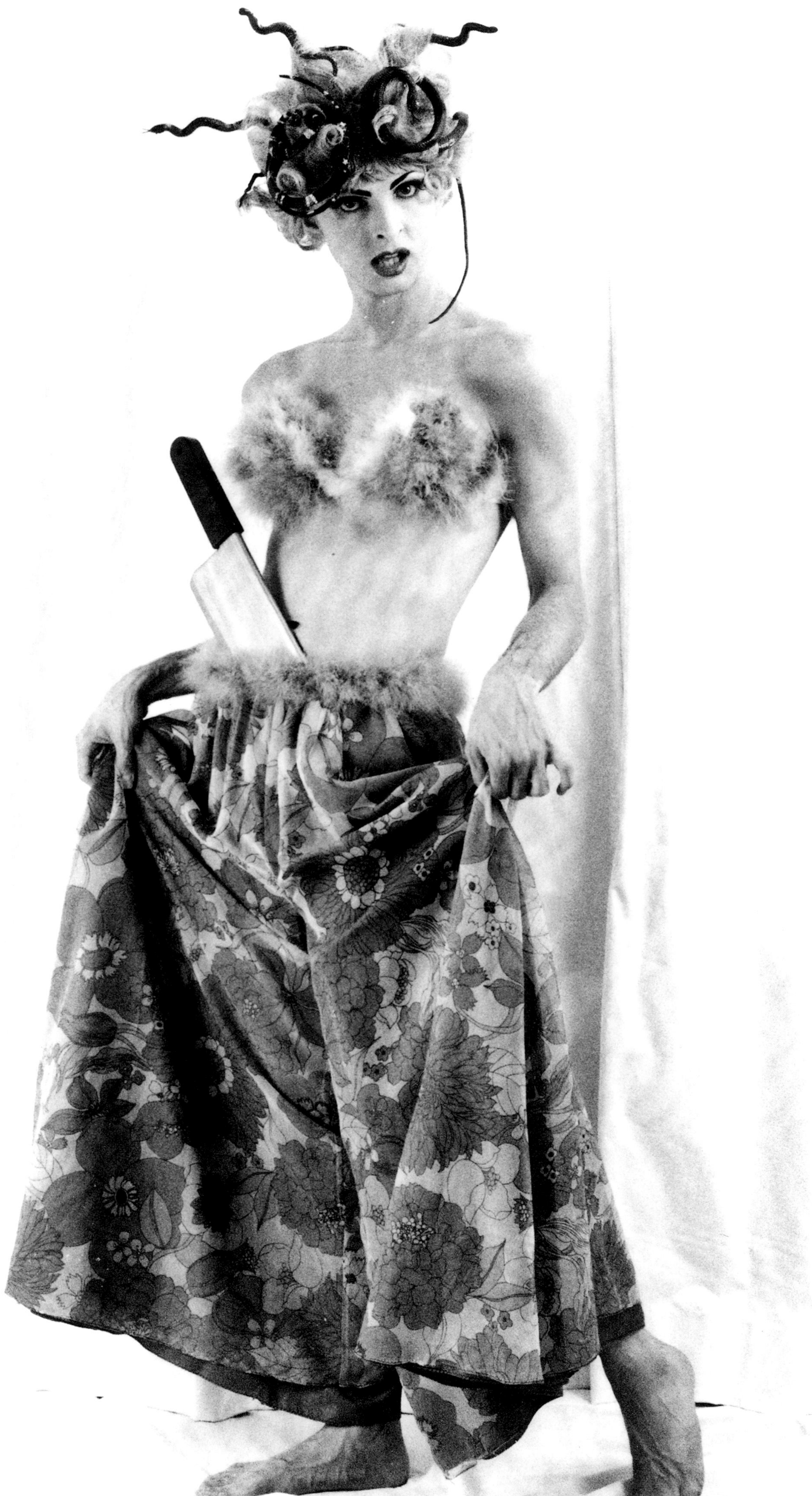

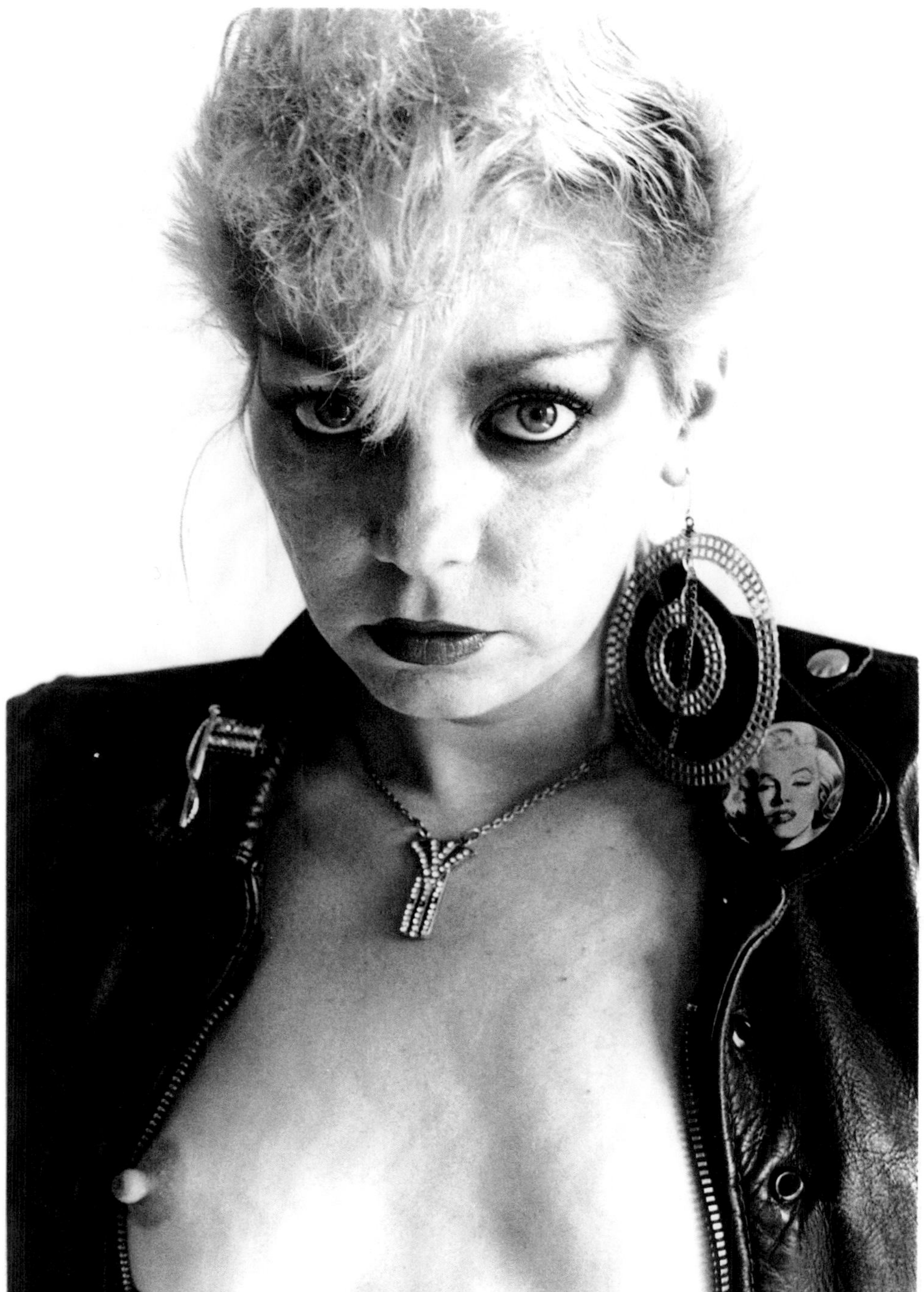

Barbara Knew she was the reincarnation of
Marilyn Monroe. She was compelled to unveil
this secret on too many social occasions and was
going to become famous in about two weeks from
the date of this photograph.

AR '85

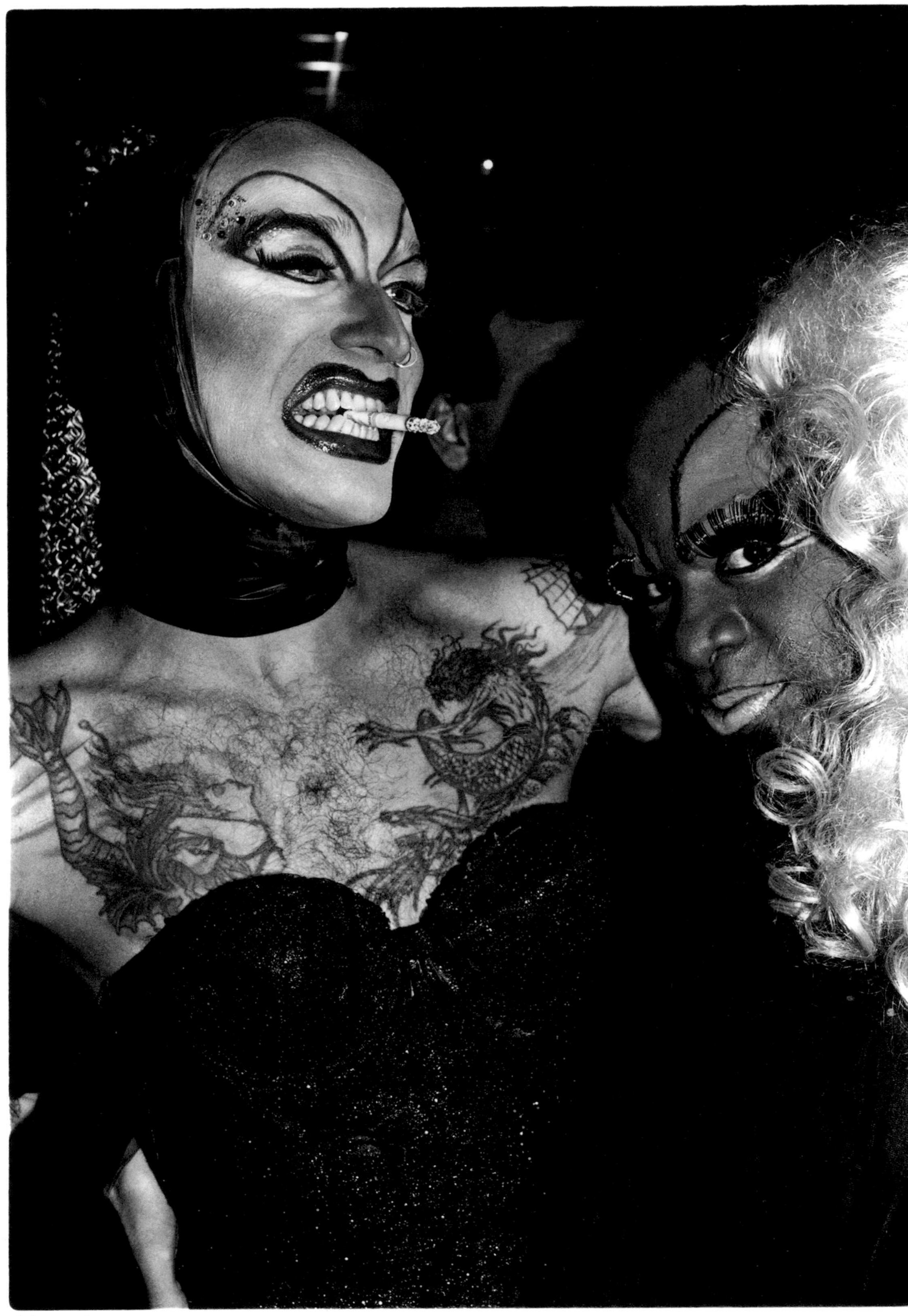

Mistress Q — and, Bebe

If it weren't for a couple of straight people, how would've your gay ass got here?

The "Lady" Bunny

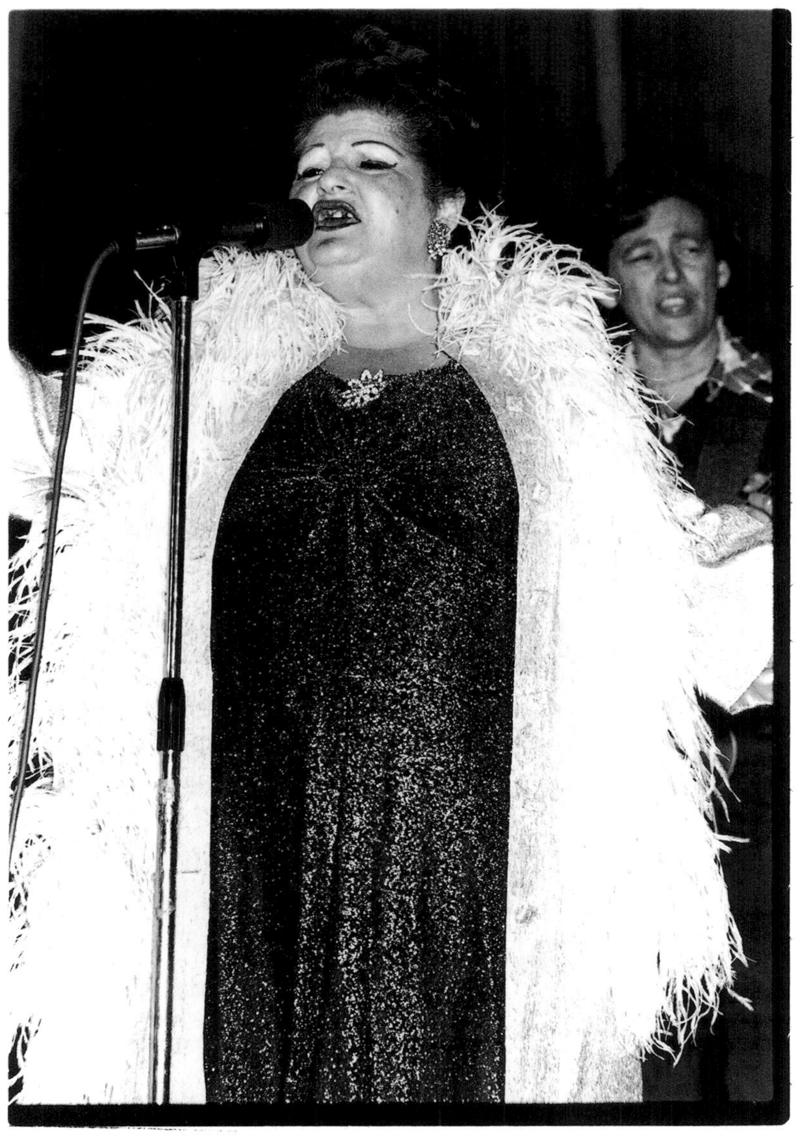

Behind Edith is Jan of the Roc-a-Jets. This was the first woman's band in Baltimore to dress like men. It was started by Jan + Jo in 1955 + Edie joined in 1959. There were no lesbian bars in Balto. at that time and as far as Baltimorians were concerned, there were no lesbians either. They played the Pepper Hill on N. Gay street between 1963–1968 and were scouted by Jimmy Dean, Jack Parr and the Grand ole Opre. They did not perform on these shows because they refused to dress feminine. They were the shock Troops of the lesbian movement in Baltimore. Jo still plays occasionally at Rumors.

AR 75

Edith Massey's singing debut at the "Denim + Pearls" ball in the Alcazar in 1975. "Rhinestone Cowgirl", "Big Girls Don't Cry", "Punks, Get off the grass": later recorded by Egg Spurt Productions in 1982.

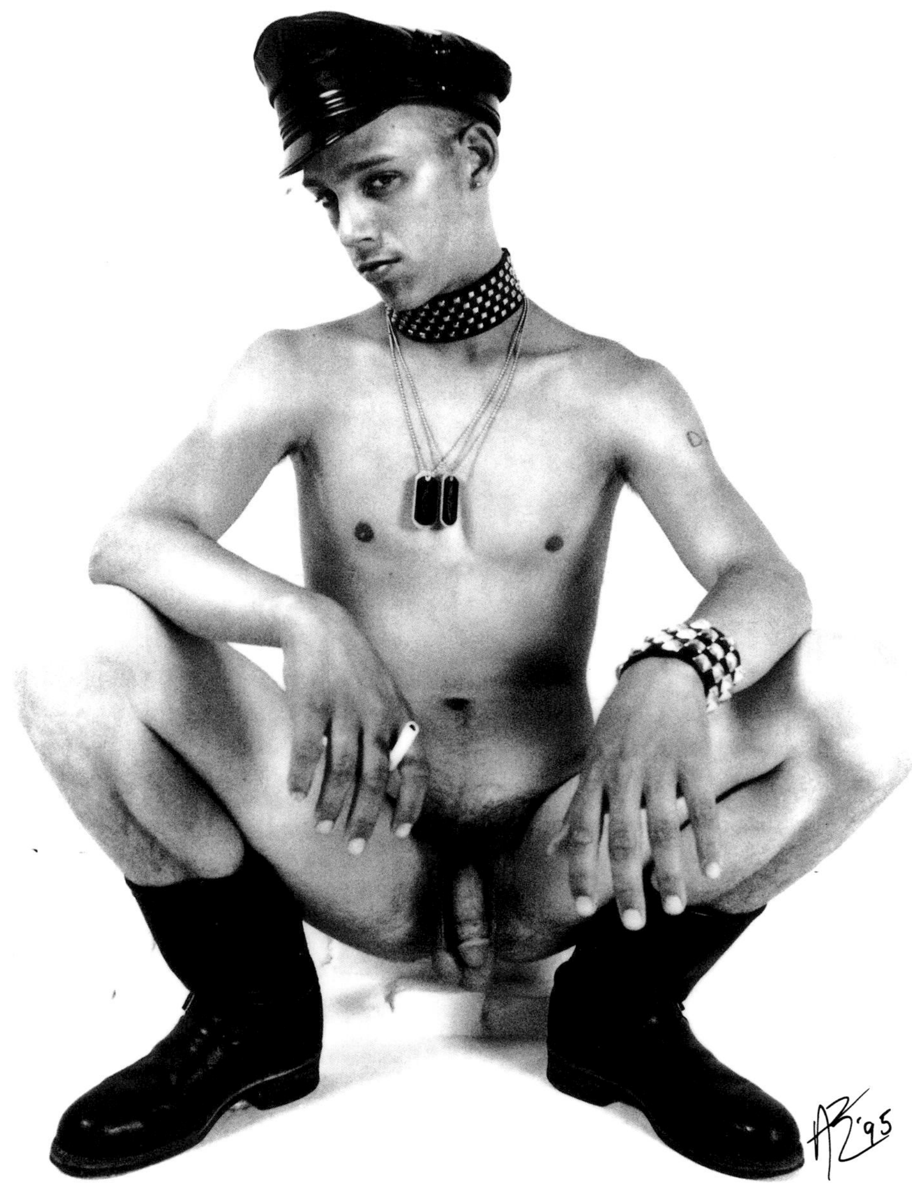

Chucky: Born, 1976.

Chucky was certainly high for this photograph. From a large family subsisting on drugs. His only son died at 4 months & his younger brother in May of 1995 at 15 of a cocaine overdose. No education. An early dependence on heroin. Always on the streets — a feverous & Byzantine art of survival. As of the summer of '98 he is doing 10 yrs. for parole violations on numerous drug charges.

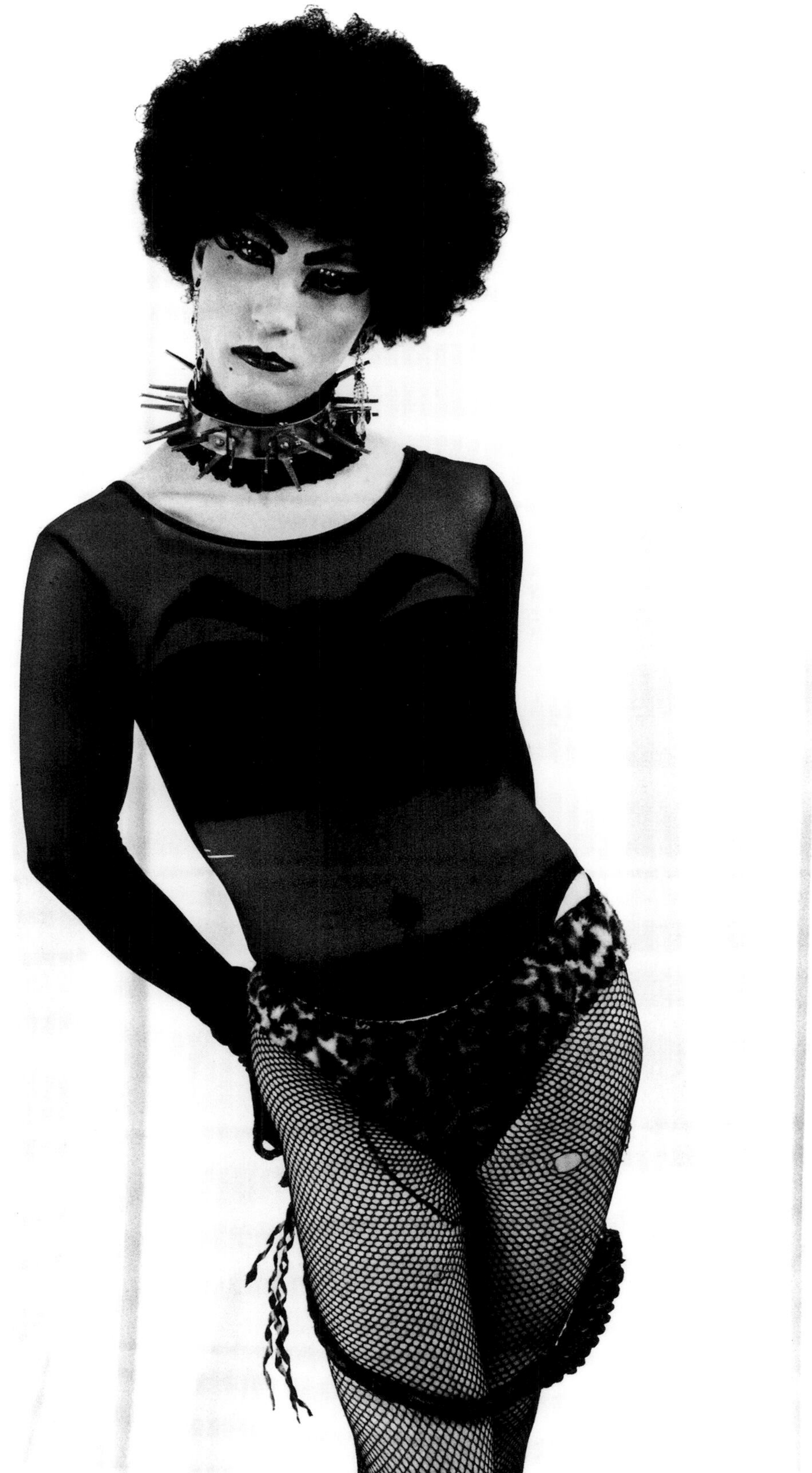

Nonamie Flowers ... of the House of Frau

the Frau Live performance of July 17, 1993,
disrupted by the Baltimore Vice Squad —
218 W. Saratoga St.

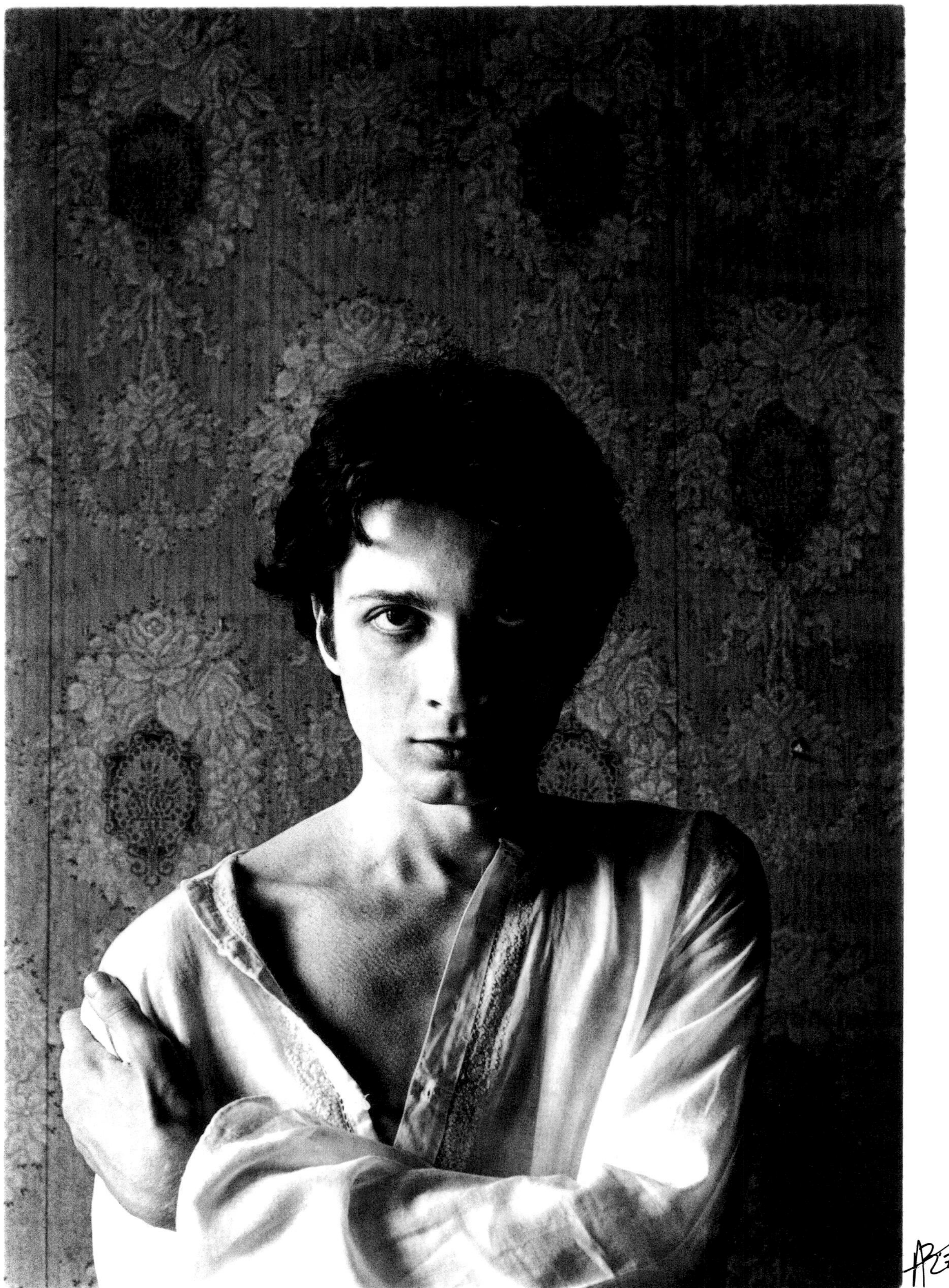

"a grief for Kenneth Palistina" by Elliott Coleman (1906–1980)

The joy of your voice
makes the telephone tremble
You have flown an ocean
and are only miles away.
All your young life is true
To the telephone ties I shall see soon.
4 white chrysanthemums
glow on the wall
each a soft clench of your fist.
Through the window bare brown trees
exhale the sunshine of 24 December.
I an old man awaiting your arrival
now feel a bottomless grief.
The chrysanthemums' whiteness dwindles.
I watch your fiery translucence
freeze into art.

24-12-77

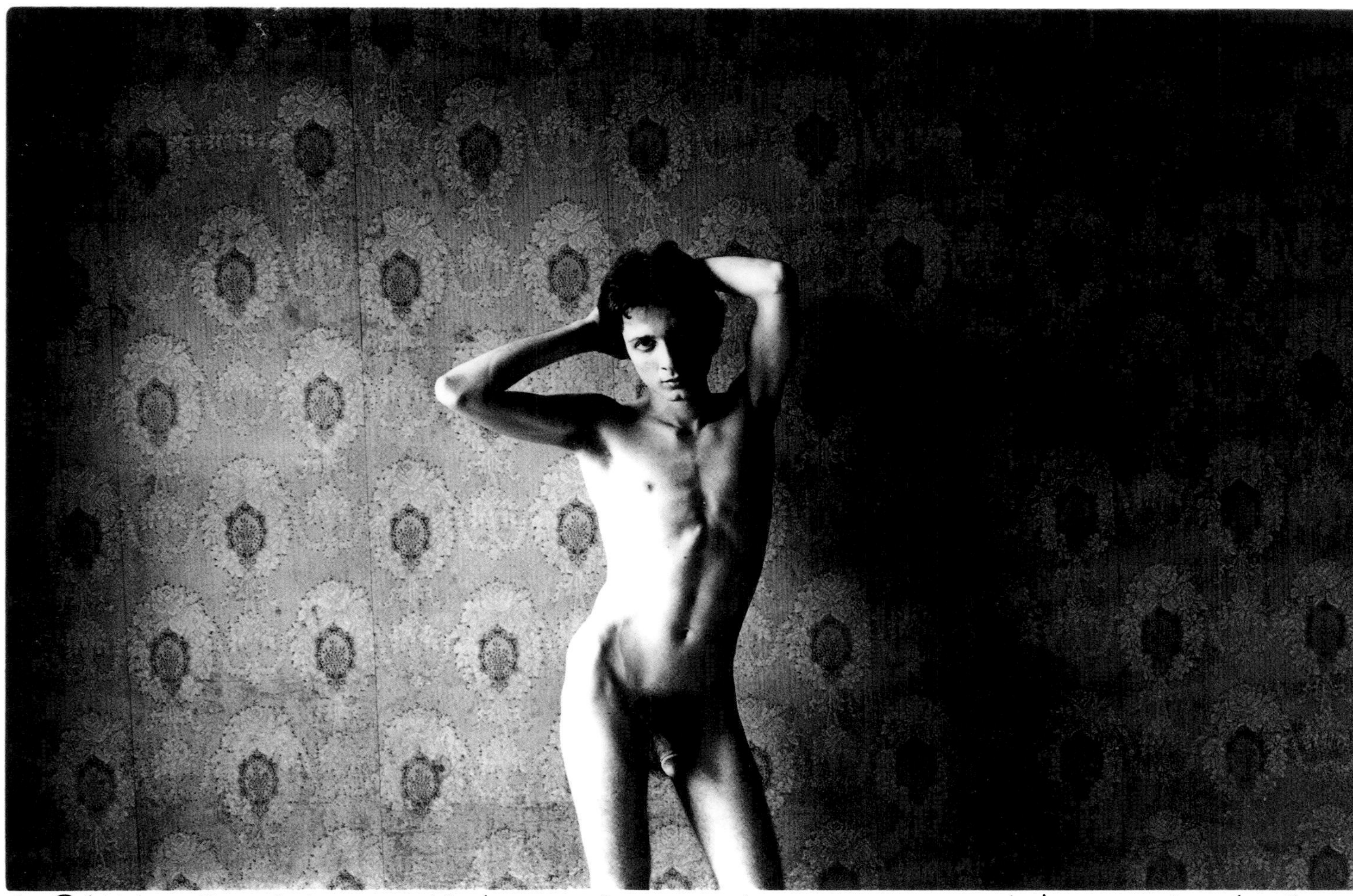

AB 76

Ken Palistina: Prose fictions, published in London 1976 – from "Communion or Why I cannot sleep alone"

"You see things when you wake alone in the hot night, the sweat drying on your skin as you lean out the casement window. Like seeing the old Italian man with thick crusty lips in the apartment next door whose kitchen window can be seen from mine who scratched 'and Mrs.' from his mail box years ago they tell me. He has white eyebrows and a large wart between his eyes where the eyebrows would meet. – He has on the table before him a sweating bottle of beer, some small red peppers, a plastic coffee cup & a spoon. His hand shaking, he slowly fills the cup with the beer drop by drop until the liquid is held an eighth inch beyond the brim by surface tension. He places one red pepper on his tongue, swallows without chewing, takes one spoonful of beer then swallows another pepper, another spoonful of beer & so on until the cup of beer is empty & the peppers are gone. – This takes as long as it takes to boil an egg & eat three jelly doughnuts or write a poem & perk coffee. Then he dries the cup with terry cloth, puts it on a shelf & sits down again resting his thumbs in his straps of his suspenders. You see things you would not see were there someone to turn over to."

Frank was born in 1955, the year I graduated from high school

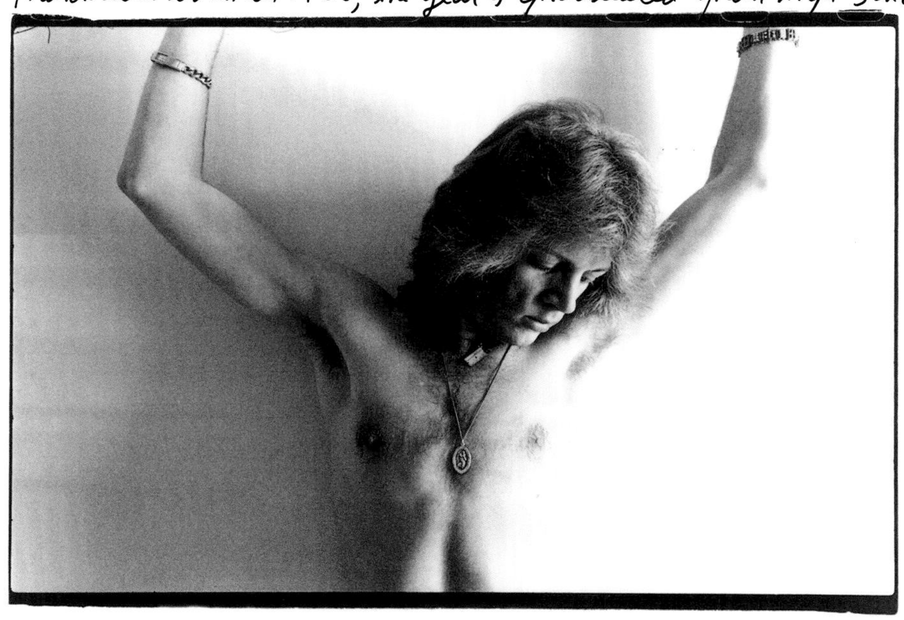

Not even a voice wafer is heard
among the stars' splintered echoes.
John Yau "Medusa"

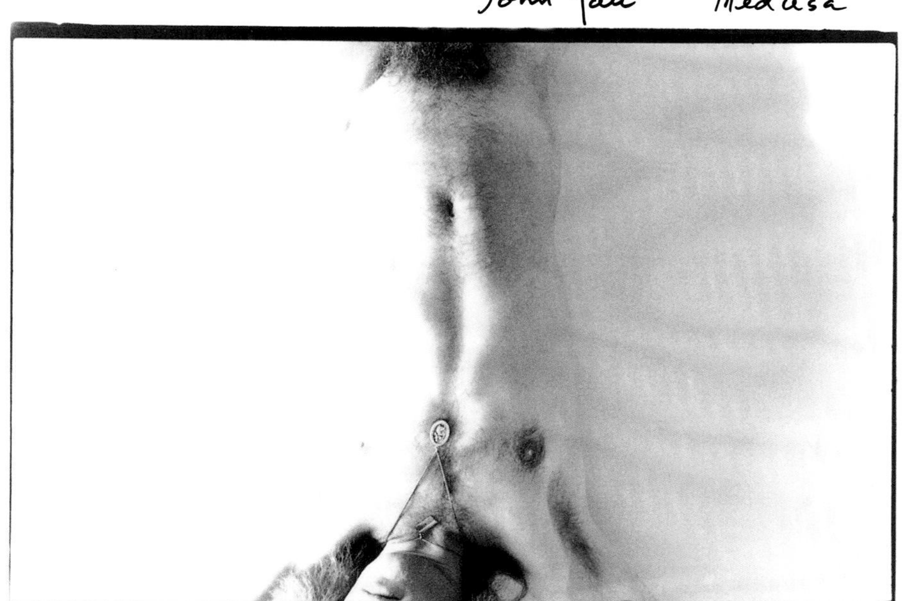

HB 75

and died in 1992 of AIDS, at 37.

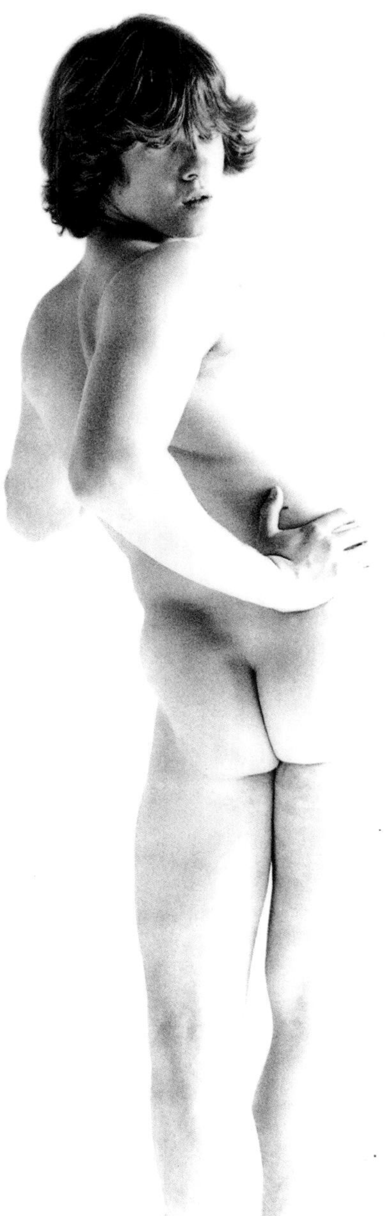

David B. '81

David was the beautifully normal, god-given, middle-class "Great American Teenager". He probably married in his twenties and voted for Reagan — and Bush. Do not expect to recognize him from this photograph.

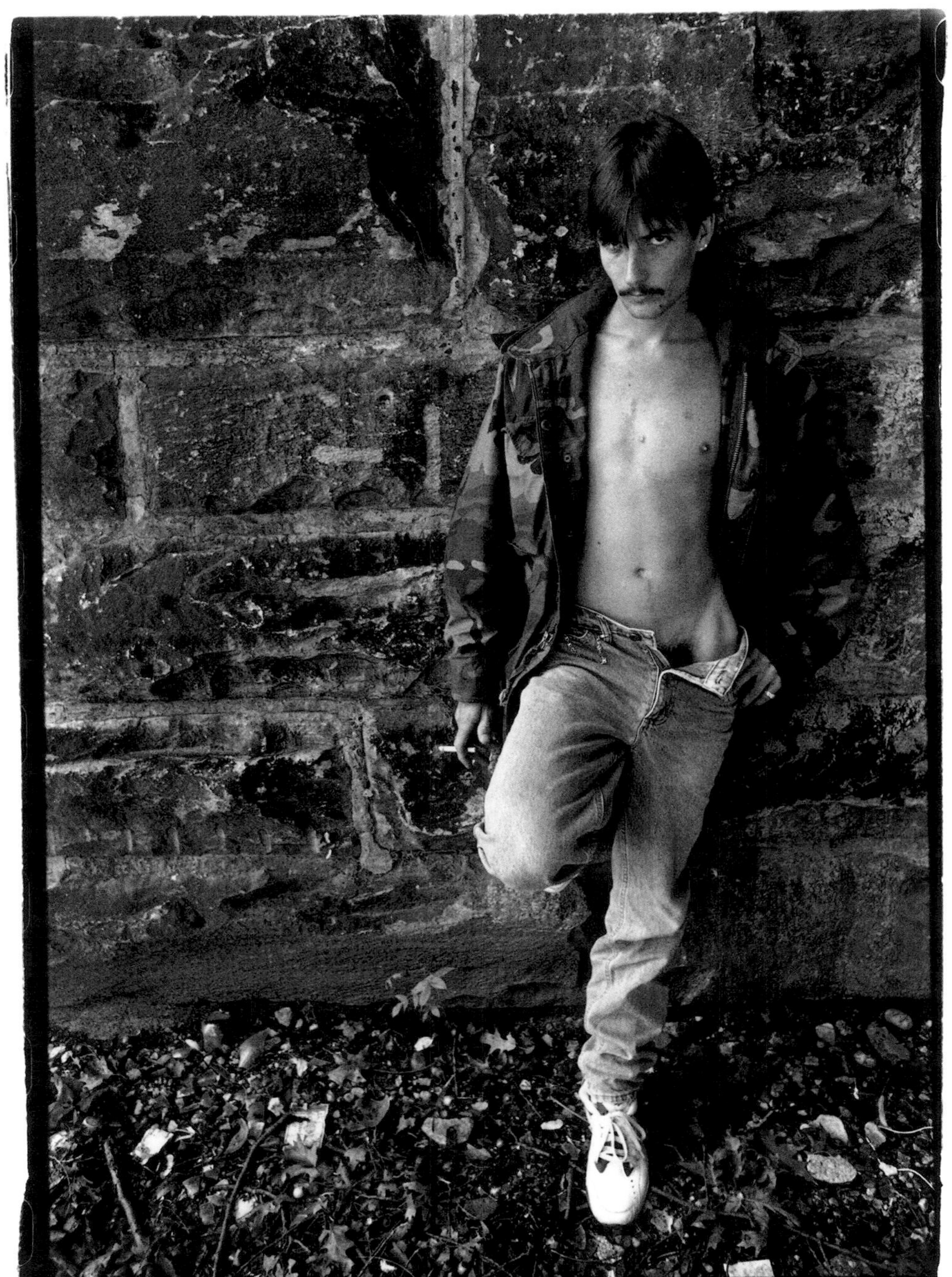

Walt MacNew

Here Walt is 24 yrs. of age. A Remington boy.
His father left the family when he was ten and the
dominant women in his life were his mother, grand-
mother & sister. Like all boys of his class he is
"straight" but has been hustling men since 14.
Or whatever else it takes to survive.

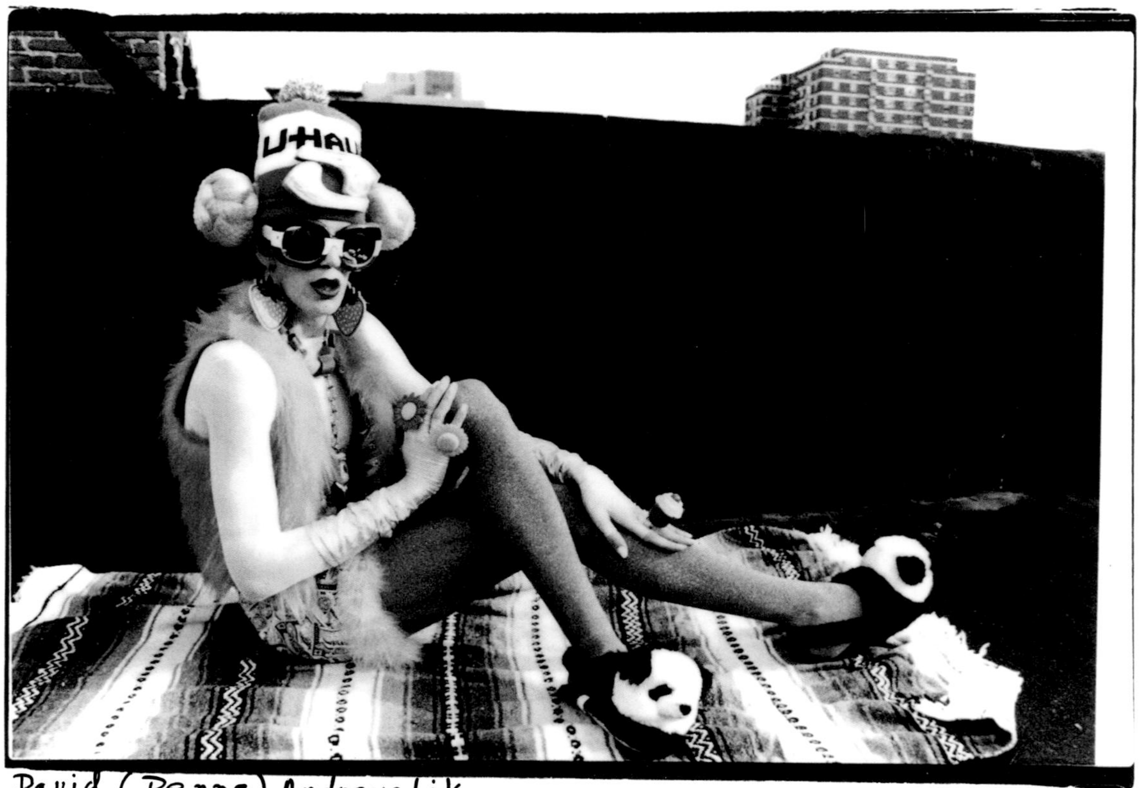

David (Denne) Andreychik

AE93

If Miss Alice had been looking a little more carefully through the looking glass, she would undoubtedly have seen Madeliny Kennedy right there with the slithy toves and the frumious Bandersnatch. Just Denne! the name most familiar to the general population, can bring a suburban shopping mall to a standstill and cardiac arrest to a construction site. Conceived under the sign of the transsexual, whatever that sign is, Denne (Madenny Fielding Carlyle) is a master of retro-syringe art, pop-condom art and the creator of gnome-like, asexual, doll lover-demons — modern succubi who people his claustraphobic Wonderland at 200 E. Preston ST. Batimore. This includes a mother and a varying number of feline companions. It does not include an air-conditioner. David was shot a few years back during a break-in — and survived. He's not running for president.

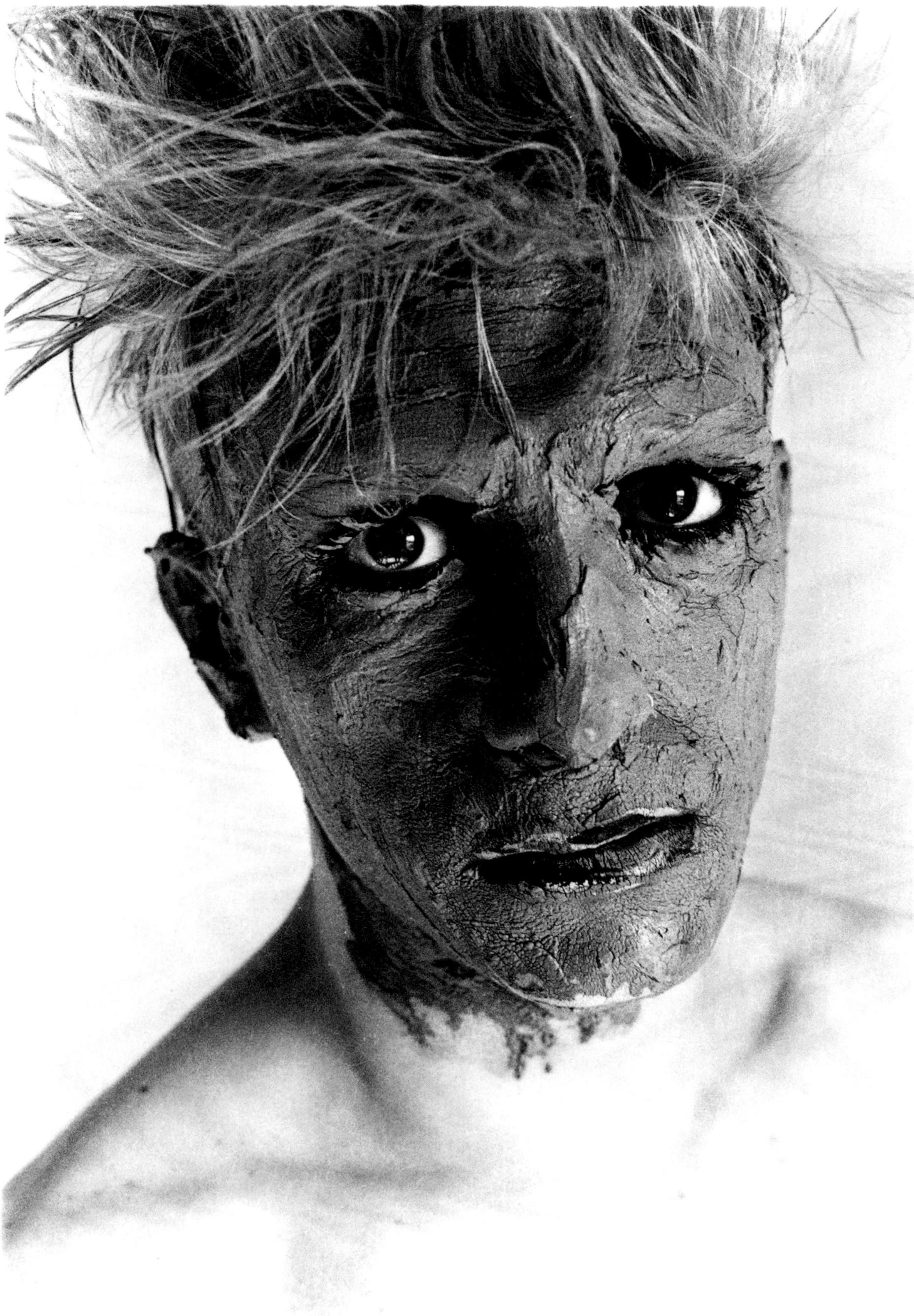

Robert Carl Nance

Bob was hardly programed to survive. Kind, exuberant, talented, fascinated by animal bones + pain. Finally drugs + heroin controlled his life, ravaged friendships + drove him beyond the borders of civilized action. He ended his life in 1992 when he was diagnosed with AIDS.

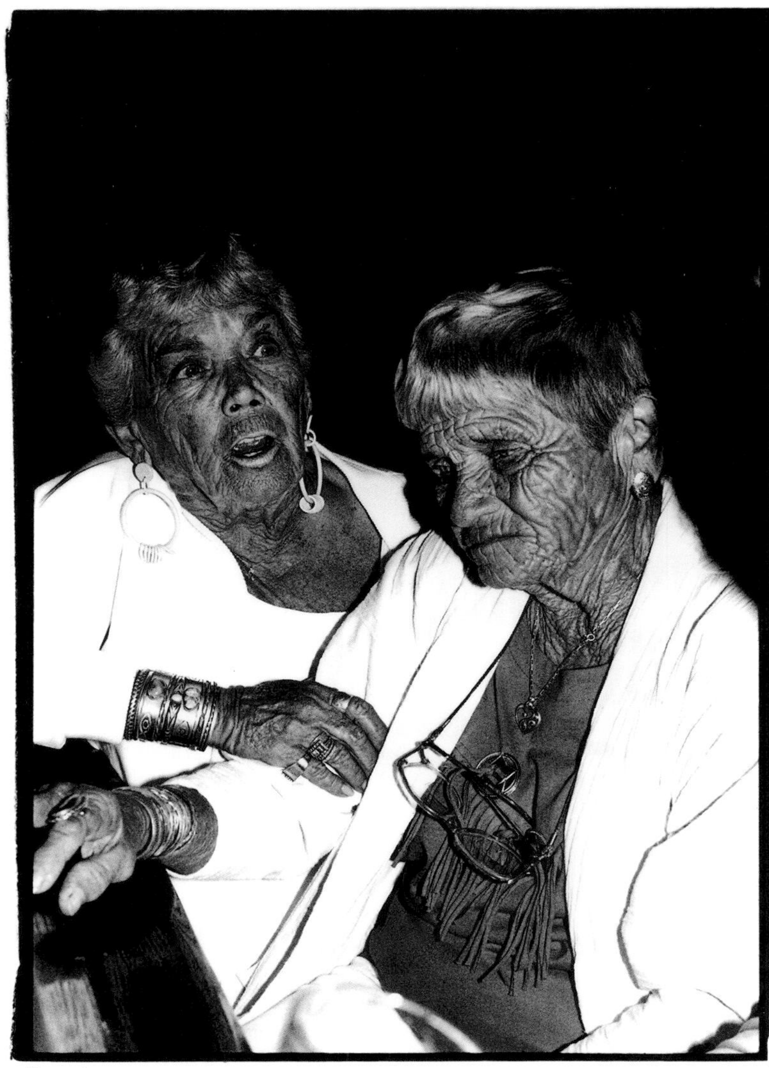

Central Station - Charles Street

Another wrinkled citizen
I have come to tell you
the sadness machine
is on the fritz again

John Yau "Cascade"

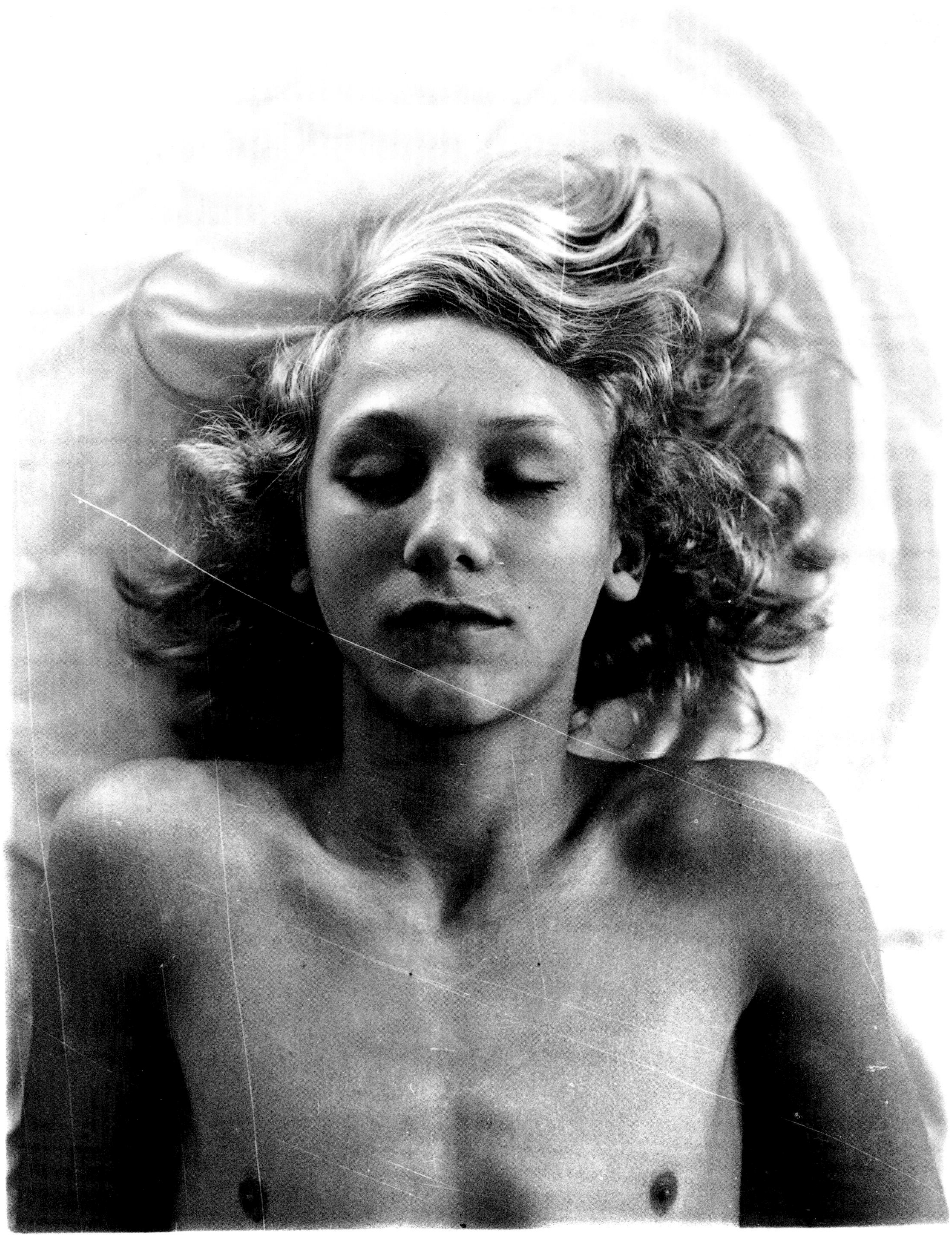

AR 75

Like the beautiful bodies of those who died before growing old,
sadly shut away in a sumptuous mausoleum,
roses by the head, jasmine at the feet—
so appear the longings that have passed
without being satisfied, not one of them granted
a single night of pleasure, or one of its radiant mornings.

C.P. Cavafy

I will tell a different story each time I am asked. On the inside of her thigh, in a ring of pink stars, is tattooed the dead actor's thumb-print, her dressmaker's initials, and a lost air micro-chip leased from a bank in Panama.

John Yau "Return of Ulysses I"

Printed in Italy on acid-free paper ∞
Design by Nancy Sears
Typography by Azalea Graphics
Printed by EBS, Editoriale Bortolazzi-Stei, Verona, Italy

Library of Congress Cataloging-in-Publication Data

Badertscher, Amos.
Baltimore portraits / Amos Badertscher : introduction by Tyler Curtain.
p. cm.
ISBN 0-8223-2334-6 (cloth : alk. paper).
ISBN 0-8223-2368-0 (paper : alk. paper).
1. Portrait photography—Maryland—Baltimore. 2. Gays—Maryland—Baltimore—Portraits. 3. Transvestites—Maryland—Baltimore—Portraits. 4. Prostitutes—Maryland—Baltimore—Portraits. 5. Baltimore (Md.)—Social life and customs—Pictorial works. 6. Badertscher, Amos.
I. Duke University. Museum of Art. II. Title.
TR680.B24 1999
779'.2'092—dc21 98-43770 CIP